The Book of
LYME REGIS

The Story of Dorset's Western Spa

RODNEY LEGG

HALSGROVE

First published in Great Britain in 2003.

British Library Cataloguing-in-Publication Data.
A CIP record for this title is available from the British Library.

ISBN 1 84114 238 7

HALSGROVE

Halsgrove House
Lower Moor Way
Tiverton, Devon EX16 6SS
Tel: 01884 243242
Fax: 01884 243325
email: sales@halsgrove.com
website: www.halsgrove.com

Frontispiece photograph: *Pilot Boat Hotel* (left) *and Bridge Street with the Fossil Depot* (centre) *and specimen on the pavement.*

Printed and bound by Bookcraft Ltd, Midsomer Norton.

Contents

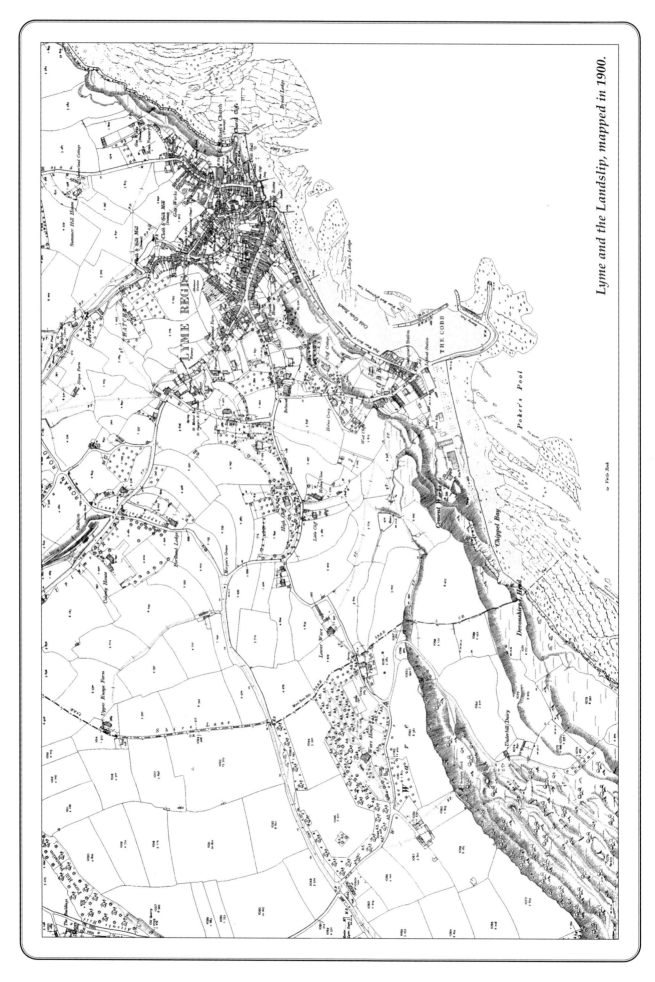

Lyme and the Landslip, mapped in 1900.

Introduction

Thanks to its Cobb harbour, as the gem in a scenic setting, Lyme is the most beautiful town in Dorset. The beneficial accident of unstable geology conspires to maintain its claim. Lyme slopes and slides towards the sea and the sun. Unsuitable developments are liable to slip into the bay as the earth yields up the best museum-standard fossils in Britain and Europe.

Lyme, with its nature-sanctuary undercliff managed by English Nature and expanses of wild National Trust land on either side of the town, provided at least half the justification for Devon and Dorset's Jurassic coast winning the ultimate accolade of World Heritage Site status. Ours is the first landscape in Great Britain to be designated by Unesco. This is where the age of the dinosaurs lives on in the cliffs. Pterodactyls remain abundant, but for me the 180-million-year-old surprise is that Lyme can boast the world's oldest moth.

This is a story of people as well as their place. Lyme's leading ladies include the novelist Jane Austen, fellow writer Mary Mitford, artificial-stone manufacturer Eleanor Coade, pioneer palaeontologist – 'fossilist' she called herself – Mary Anning, plant-protector Lady Muriel Abbot-Anderson, cinema pianist Nellie Templeton and dramatist Ann Jellicoe.

My balancing list of seven of its menfolk who have done most for the benefit of humanity are philanthropist Thomas Coram, life-saver and novelist Frederick Marryat, inventor of the self-bouyant lifeboat Sir Richard Spencer, bird discoverer and illustrator John Gould, antiseptic surgeon Sir Joseph Lister, child psychologist Alexander Sutherland Neill, and international novelist and local museum curator John Fowles.

Many others will join this personal choice as the chronology unfolds. It will close with a top ten, which literally ring out over the town, as they are the world-record-holding bells in St Michael's Parish Church. Their names and inscriptions incorporate national, town and bell-ringing history. The tenth carries the name of John Davy Hodder. It was a timely reminder to me to do justice to the town's sea sagas, culminating in the lifeboat annals, and cover the history of heroism offshore.

'Lyme from Holm Bush in 1860', looking east, with Cobb Gate Jetty (centre) still a substantial projection.

*The Royal Field Artillery halt in Broad Street for an overnight stop
en route to manoeuvres on Dartmoor in 1888.*

Chapter 1

RELICS, ROMANS, ROUTES & RIDGEWAYS

Lyme as we know it evolved from a Saxon renaissance after the Dark Ages. There are significant, older, visible traces in the landscape which show that this frontier district was an area of former wealth and importance. Most of the chert-topped hills on the border lands of Devon and Dorset have their Iron-Age hill-forts. Pilsdon Pen, on the inland side of the Marshwood Vale, crowns the highest point in Dorset at 908 feet above sea level. Multiple ramparts enclose a plateau settlement with a gold-making forge and Celtic temple of the Durotriges tribe. It and contemporary earthworks on nearby Lambert's Castle Hill are owned by the National Trust. As is Coney's Castle, with stout single banks of a little earlier in the Iron Age, where 86 acres of wild land overlooking Charmouth and the English Channel were bought in 1975 with a bequest from Mrs Katharine Olive Pass, the widow of Captain Douglas Pass of Wootton Fitzpaine, who climbed it daily at the start of the First World War to scan the horizon with field-glasses on the lookout for invading Germans. Westwards, in the Iron Age, was the territory of the Dumnonii of Devon and Cornwall with Musbury Castle, south-west of Axminster, being the final frontier fort. Though in Devon, it lies on the Dorset side of the River Axe and dates from a century or so before Emperor Claudius ordered the invasion of Britain.

Roman Lyme is represented by a villa two miles away, at Holcombe on the Devon side of the border, on a flat-topped hill above Cannington Lane. Its main, or final, development included an elaborate fourth-century bathhouse with an octagonal plunge bath. Mosaics, columns and a dome with scallop-shell decoration showed an opulent lifestyle.

The antiquarian James Davidson, writing in 1833, recorded that in Holcombe Bottom:

... in the parish of Uplyme, which is skirted by a road, a man, some years ago, employed in removing a large heap of stones, provincially termed 'a stone-burrow,' discovered a very large number of Roman coins, which he carried to Exeter for sale.

Such finds were relatively common, though most were consigned to the melting-pot, as with a Celtic gold torc found beneath an Uplyme gatepost in 1817. When Cosmo the Third, Grand Duke of Tuscany, spent a night in Axminster in 1669 he was shown a collection of locally found ancient coins by the vicar, Revd J.J. Crabbe. Another hoard, of 22 silver denarii, was found at Shellacres, Higher Wyld, in 1818. Davidson inspected and identified the half that were in 'tolerable preservation' as belonging to the reigns of Vespasian (1), Domitian (1), Trajan (1), Antoninus Pius (5), Trajan (1), Lucilla, wife of Lucius Aurelius Verus (1), and Marcia Otacilia Severa, wife of Julius Philippus (1). The other one that Davidson could personally vouch for, from a depth of two feet in the churchyard at Axminster in 1830, was a bronze coin of the Emperor Claudius II with Victory on the reverse.

It is appropriate that Emperor Vespasian starts the roll-call. As commander of the Second Legion (Augusta) he conquered Dorset after the invasion of AD43, and established the Fosse Way to delineate the first frontier of the Province of Britannia, northwards from a military port at Axmouth. This may have been called Moridunum – Celtic for 'sea fortress' – and its road headed for Ilchester. Here it skirted the Somerset Levels and went on, north-eastwards, to Bath. The new frontier effectively followed the existing Iron-Age border between the Durotriges and Dumnonii. Dorchester was established as the new tribal capital with Exeter following after final resistance in the Celtic fringes had been subdued.

From later in the first century the Roman main road from Dorchester to Exeter crossed Lyme's hinterland via Hogchester and Street Wood – both names indicating the Roman link – to pass the former Penn Inn before crossing the top of the hills beside Hunter's Lodge Inn at Burrowshot Cross. Its onward course, over Greenway Head, was in line with the eighteenth-century turnpike road down into Axminster. Here it crossed the River Axe at Bow Bridge. That was its route but the tumbling terrain of the hills, rising out of the Marshwood Vale, makes much of the central course imprecise. Westwards, however, there can be no doubt. Near Honiton and at Rockbeare are well-preserved sections of the agger or causeway, complete with flanking side ditches.

Lyme's own ancient lost road, a prehistoric ridgeway which stayed busy in the Roman period, can be traced across the top of the East Devon cliffs from Axmouth, Dowlands, Whitlands, Pinhay and Lower Ware.

Coney's Castle (left) and Lambert's Castle Hill (right) combine to form a National Trust skyline of ancient earthworks above Lyme Regis.

The Iron-Age rampart at Lambert's Castle rings a hilltop enclosure that was reused for a beacon, semaphore station and fairground.

Pilsdon Pen, the highest point in Dorset and the biggest of the western hill-forts, also overlooks Lyme's hinterland.

Plateau ramparts of Pilsdon Pen, at 908 feet above sea level, looking south to Lyme Bay (centre).

Tumbling countryside near Birdsmoor Gate where the road from Crewkerne to Lyme climbs to cross Lambert's Castle Hill.

Gorse-covered Iron-Age ramparts at Coney's Castle.

Into Dorset and across the town its course is clear, as Clappentail Lane and the Roman Road which crosses the River Lim by Horn Bridge – named for the former Horn Tavern – and then climbs away as Colway Lane and Timber Hill into National Trust land at the Spittles. Here its line for half a mile fell into landslipped inaccessibility in the 1920s, although it resumes at the Devil's Bellows as Old Lyme Hill which descends into Charmouth. Joining it here is the Old Lyme Road, which was the first turnpike route into Lyme in 1768. Before about 1750 the main route inland from Lyme was the 'via regia' or King's Highway beside the River Lim, from Coombe Street to Uplyme, and the main road at Hunter's Lodge Inn.

The most lavish Roman find from the Devon-Dorset border lands, picked up on Seaton beach in 1840, was a second-century Mediterranean bronze of Achilles as a boy riding Chiron the centaur. It either came from the settlement at Seaton or an ancient shipwreck offshore.

Above: *Charmouth (right) and Lyme Regis (centre) in a study by Colin Graham, south-westwards from Hardown Hill, in 1985.*

Left: *The former coast road between Lyme Regis and Charmouth in 1910, before being destroyed by landslips and subsidence, looking eastwards to Golden Cap (top right).*

11

*All that remains of the old road eastwards towards Charmouth, from Timber Hill,
photographed by Colin Graham in 1985.*

**Lyme's wild and empty eastern cliffs – the
Spittles and Black Ven – and a glimpse of
Charmouth (right) north-east from
Church Cliffs in 1998.**

Lyme's setting (top right), south-westwards from Black Ven wilderness, with mud sliding across Canary Ledges (centre) in 1996.

Warning notice on a National Trust gate which applies to the entire coastal landscape between Lyme and Charmouth.

Turnpike milestone above Lyme Regis at the midway point between Axminster and Bridport.

West Dorset's own Saxon saint, complete with relics and shrine, is Saint Wite at Whitchurch Canonicorum.

Chapter 2

MEDIEVAL ROYAL BOROUGH & PORT

The focus of civilisation on what had become the borders of Devon and Dorset moved eastwards and Lyme received its earliest documentary mention in 774. King Cynewulf granted land on the west bank of the River Lim to the Bishop of Sherborne. There the great church was a cathedral before it became an abbey. The link is with what is now the Sherborne Lane area of Lyme and the economic reason for the land deal was salt-panning.

The Parish Church of St Michael the Archangel, now poised on Church Cliff but originally a safe distance inland, has a tower with a Saxon core, although it was revamped by the Normans in about 1120. Repairs to it over the winter of 1994 revealed an earlier window, dating from around AD980, in the south wall of the ringing-chambers on the first floor. It is therefore quite possible that all but the top third comprises what is still, basically, Saxon masonry. This tower was originally at the west end of the

Saxon building and then in the centre of a Norman cruciform. Expansions of 1320 and 1500 were eastwards, into a big nave, and westwards with a porch. What remains of the archaeology of its Norman north and south aisles lies under the disturbed grass of the graveyard on either side of the two visible base sections of the tower walls.

To the south-west, the tiny river and its Buddle estuary were too shallow and rocky to be a safe haven for vessels, other than those that could be hauled out of the water. On the other hand, it did afford some protection on an exposed coast of wild, scrubby cliffs. The original Buddle Bridge, a Norman structure across what was then a much wider estuary, incorporated a priest's chamber where pre-Reformation monks collected salt dues and bridge tolls.

The room, remains of which were discovered on the south-west side in 1913, was mentioned in the will of wealthy merchant John Tudbold who died in 1548.

St Michael's Parish Church, from the north-west, in 1906.

The church, looking inland from the south-east, in 1997.

He describes 'a Chamber in which our Lady's Priest sometime dwelled', located near the pre-1844 Customs House in the Square, 'and lying next to the Bridge of Lyme aforesaid.' Tudbold left it to the town, although his initial wish would have been spiked by Henry VIII's suppression of the religious houses:

I commit [it] to the discretion of the Mayor for the time being and his Brethren to bestow it as they shall think best, for a Priest if they shall have any serving our Lady's Service, or else to bestow it on two poor people.

The most detailed architectural account of the remains of the bridge is the report of an inspection made by civil engineer Charles Beresford Fox in 1911:

It consists of one arch in the pointed Gothic style, giving a clear span of 15 feet at the springing level some five feet above the bed; and rising to a total height of 15 feet 6 inches. Originally, four masonry ribs, 17 inches, of cut and chamfered stone, 3 feet 6 inches apart centre to centre and rising almost imperceptibly out of the receding abutments, supporting the main arch over its full width of 13 feet; but today only two of these ribs are intact – namely, that nearest the up-stream face and the next but one. The intermediate rib is replaced by two curved timbers abutting at the soffit, while that which existed furthest down-stream is entirely gone.

Above and between the ribs, the arch is composed of rough limestone masonry filled in with later brick and mortar, but is faced both up and down-stream by similar hewn and chamfered stone replaced by voussoir stones of longer length where repairs required. From a study of these ribs it appears to have been built about the year 1400. An old wooden house and fish shop, spanning the river on three old timbers, abuts the bridge on the down-stream side, this not only obviating all necessity of a parapet but completely hiding the bridge from the sea.

A view of this ancient work may, however, be obtained from a point some 40 yards up-stream, or by permission of the occupier of the first house on the left past the bridge, where it may be seen from a back door opening out to a flight of steps leading down to the water's edge, and where formerly no doubt many a load of contraband goods was disembarked at night on the top of the tide.

Buddle was a Dorset-dialect word for a 'choked trough', which would have described the natural geography of the Lim's entry into the sea, like the River Char at Charmouth and the River Winniford at Seatown, trickling through a bank of shingle. The River Lim also acted as the town's sewer and the fetid pool behind the shingle continued to give offence until the first sea walls were built after 1750.

To the east, Broad Ledge jutted out to sea, and immediately to the south-west another spit

High and dry Lim estuary and the Buddle Bridge, with buildings on it, prior to their demolition in 1911.

An angry sea beside the Buddle estuary (left) and Gun Cliff lookout and battery (centre), with Golden Cap beyond (centre right), painted by Charles Marshall from Cobb Gate Jetty in 1832.

Gun Cliff (left) *and the steps down to the Buddle estuary, looking eastwards from the Square in 1927, to Cain's Folly* (centre) *and Golden Cap* (right).

Church Beach, with the Curtis family's lobster-pots seen in the 1880s in a view south-westwards to Gun Cliff and the Buddle, when it was Lyme's eastern fishery.

extended much further seawards than at present. It was here, between Cobb Gate and Cobb Gate Beach, that a fishing hamlet grew up with boat-hauls on the east-facing side. This became the first Cobb harbour – defined by boulders cleared from the estuary –

semi-sheltered and backed by an exposed sliver of buildings, comprising boathouses, warehouses and homes.

Lyme's connection with Sherborne was confirmed by a Papal Bull, signed in Rome by Pope Eugenius III

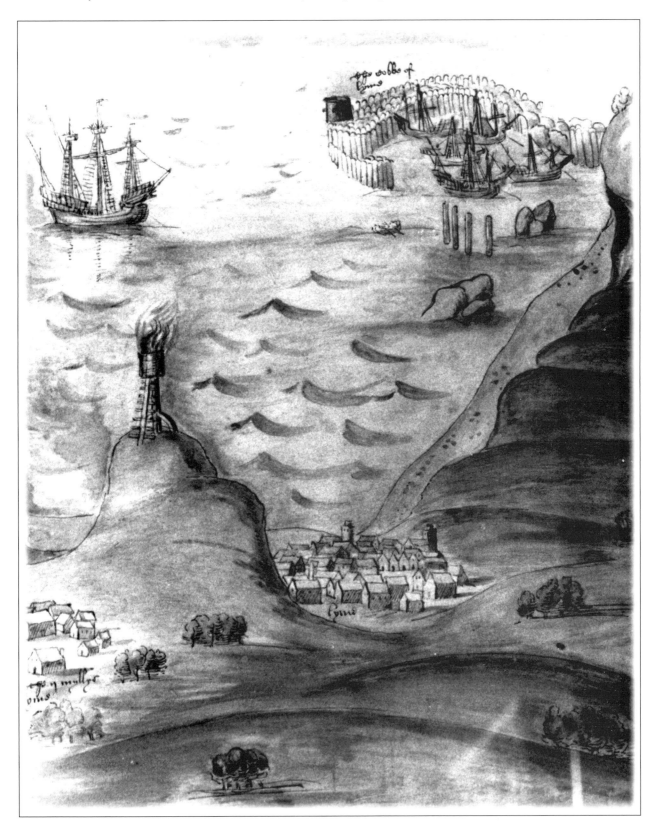

Armada period pictorial map showing 'the Cobb of Lyme' (top), Lyme Regis town (centre), Charmouth (left), and a blazing beacon on Timber Hill.

Lyme's oldest street, Sherborne Lane,
with sash-windows in 1904.

Rustic section of Sherborne Lane,
north-westwards down steps to
Gosling Bridge and Angel Inn,
in 1905.

in 1145, which codified the granting of Lyme and its fishing rights to the Abbot of Sherborne. The merchants of Lyme found new wealth in the five years after 1152 when Eleanor of Aquitaine, divorcee of King Louis VII of France, married Henry of Anjou who is better known as King Henry II of England. The match caused the ceding to England of the Aquitaine province to which Eleanor was heiress. Outgoing cargoes of West Country timber were exchanged in Bordeaux for fine wine from the Garonnne and Gascogne.

Gilbert of London, acting on a commission from King Henry III in 1261, required the Bailiffs of Lyme to provide vessels to carry Queen Eleanor and Prince Edward to France. As a result, the royal cachet, Regis, was bestowed on the Dorset town of Lyme by King Edward (I) in 1284. Lyme was declared a 'free borough' with its citizens being 'free burgesses' who could establish a merchants' guild and enjoy other liberties 'without let or hindrance of the justices, sheriffs, bailiffs, or any other officers for ever.'

Lyme's first Market Street, later called West Street, is now Broad Street which branches at Top of Town into Silva Street, subsequently Silver Street (from the medieval Latin for its wooded backdrop), and Pound Street, named for the edge-of-town enclosure where animals found straying or grazing without authority on manorial common land were impounded. Gosling Bridge at the northern end of Sherborne Lane and the Lynch, dating from Tudor times or earlier, marked the northern boundary of the royal borough.

The Lynch, downstream from the Angel Inn beside the River Lim, looking north-westwards in 1910.

Bridge Street after widening in 1913 with the Parish Church rising above the Pilot Boat Hotel.

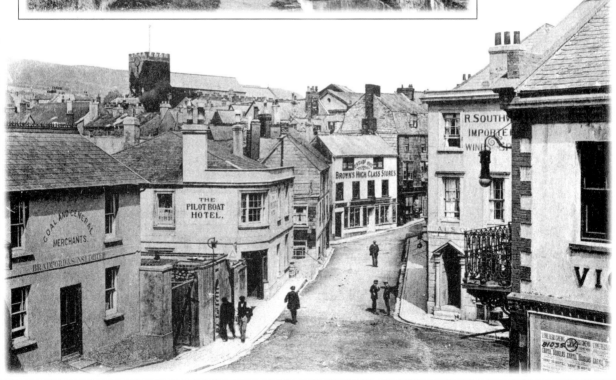

The River Lim and the Lynch, northwards to the Angel Inn, in 1997.

The so-called Lepers' Well, under the arch, in a view south-westwards from the Lynch towards Broad Street which lies over the hill.

Two burgesses of the free borough of Lyme Regis were summoned by the King in 1295 to attend the calling of the earliest regular Parliament. Geoffrey le Keu and William de Tholuse were the town's first MPs. Their presence shows the importance of the town and also marked the beginning of the gradual and grudging transfer of power from the monarch to the people. By 1308 the members of Parliament had turned themselves from a debating chamber into a legislative assembly whose assent was a prerequisite to the making of law. That period, as witnessed by John de Sutton who was representing Lyme in 1348, arguably saw the establishment of democracy in England.

The names of the townsmen, initially representing places of ancestry, as in William de Tholuse – William of Toulouse – evolved from local locations and the landscape. William le Gate was probably William from the Bridge, which in Lyme's case has him living beside the Buddle estuary. John atte Mulle was a miller, William le Smith a blacksmith, William le Portreve the officer of the port, and Adam le Mercer a cloth merchant. John le Skynnere worked at the tannery and Nicholas Pistorius is but a Latinisation of the same trade as Nigel Baker. These names were extracted by historian Cyril Wanklyn from the town's mentions in one of the earliest of paper manuscripts – as distinct from vellum parchments on goat skins – who points out that a mix of Latin and medieval English names can have John le Poletarius and John le Polter appearing as one and the same poulterer just a few lines apart. The town's Court Book was given to the British Museum by Corscombe rector Revd William Maskell whose second wife was the daughter of John Stein of Highcliff in Lyme. They moved on to Bude Castle and Maskell died in 1890 in Penzance.

Lyme's first harbour, such as it was, evolved into a commercial complex of dwellings and warehouses on a tongue of land running seawards from the present Cobb Gate Jetty, on the south side of the Square at the bottom of Broad Street. It seems to have extended seawards for about 150 yards. This was the ancient Cobb and there is no evidence that the present one, half a mile away, was built in its original scythe-like shape before the end of the fourteenth century.

Vessels from Lyme were turning up all around north-western Europe, as various foreign records show, with *Our Lady of Lyme* in particular – as *Notre Dame de Lim* – carrying the flag on charter to the Baltic ports in 1322. Out at sea there was open rivalry between vessels from Lyme and Dartmouth which broke into the 'enormous transgressions' of what sound like pitched battles.

In about 1340 a leper asylum and infirmary, dedicated to St Mary and the Holy Spirit, was established in Broad Street on the site of the Great House. Research by John Fowles has shown that its commemoration by Lepers' Well Garden, 100 yards to the north-west, is 'a recent romantic invention'. There a stone structure around a spring stands on a stream-side terrace, above the River Lim between Coombe Street and the Angel Inn. Behind the modern stonework there is an ancient arch. The spring gave its name to Fountain Garden and was carried by a medieval aqueduct eastwards across the River Lim, to Lynch Walk and the oldest part of the town. The spoiling of the myth comes as a disappointment as only one such well has survived in England, in Winchester, and that is dedicated to St Mary Magdalene.

Lyme's national importance was acknowledged in 1342 when two of its 'better and discreter mariners' were summoned to Parliament in Westminster to advise on ways to improve the production of ships for the wars in Scotland and France. The port also made its military contribution, considerable in terms of its population, by supplying four ships and 62 seamen for the siege of Paris in 1347.

They returned with the invisible scourge of Europe. Increasingly cosmopolitan seagoing brought the realisation that diseases travelled with people. By 1349, fear of the Black Death, spreading as a plague across Europe, caused the order to be sent to Lyme and other ports that no one was to disembark at English harbours other than merchants or accredited messengers.

The turning-point in Lyme's development as a port came with a devastating gale on 11 November 1377, when the original Cobb, extending seawards from Cobb Gate Jetty, was washed away by 'the horrible flux and reflux of the deep sea rolling up into the town.' A total of 77 dwellings were lost, together with warehouses and the quay. The result was a decision to build the next breakwater from the rocks beside Poker's Pool, in the south-western extremity of the town's inner bay, and to curve it around into what – with a transferred name – became the new and present Cobb. It grew slowly, with a sign of the times being that one of the first buildings was a quarantine facility that could function if necessary as an isolation hospital. Harbour building proved to be far from a precise science and the uneven struggle against the sea was still being lost a century later.

The burgesses of Lyme petitioned King Edward IV in 1481 that the town was being 'wasted by the tides and the overflowing of the sea.' Inhabitants departed after the port 'was by tempest destroyed'. The King responded favourably by granting the town freedom from 'fee-farm' taxation for a period of 65 years. It was a repaired quay and pier of stone, jutting into the sea 'for the succour of ships', that John Leland described in 1540. He noted that merchants from Morlaix, in Brittany, 'much haunt this town'.

Despite the scale of Lyme's problems, in local terms it was still in the ascendancy, as the nearby estuaries at Charmouth and Bridport Haven were no longer regarded as navigable. In 1558 it was decreed that they would in future be treated as creeks and put under the jurisdiction of Lyme Regis.

Eastern Lyme, from Church Cliffs and Church Street to Rose Nursery, looking south-westwards to the Cobb at high tide in 1895.

Below: Cobb Gate (centre) and Bell Cliff (right) south-westwards to the Cobb (left).

Marine Parade, looking along the old cart-track from the town to the Cobb in 1902.

North-eastern view, out through the harbour entrance from the Cobb to the Parish Church (centre),
painted in the 1840s.

Four trading vessels beside the Cobb quay and two yachts under sail,
with the old Lifeboat Station in the foreground in the 1880s.

The Cobb from the western cliffs in 1903.

Eastern side of the Cobb from above Marine Parade in 1912.

The Cobb building and Granny's Teeth steps (right) *in 1925.*

Cobb buildings looking south-westwards from the southern side of the harbour entrance in 1996.

The beach between Church Cliffs and the Spittles in a print by J.M.W. Turner, featuring a shipwreck with seamen and wreckage being washed ashore.

Cobb Gate Beach below Marine Parade in 1910.

Timeless scene of fishing nets beside the Cobb, with these dating from 1997, in a view north-eastwards into the centre of the town.

The inner side of the harbour at the Cobb, photographed by John Moly in 1865.

Coasters in the Cobb harbour in 1890 with a timber pier carrying the rails of a tramway.

Cobb from the cliffs to the north-west with three double-masted vessels in the 1890s.

The Cobb from Langmoor Gardens in 1912.

Calm sea on a misty morn looking north-eastwards towards the town and Parish Church (middle left) in a classic Colin Graham study from 1975.

A closer view of the Cobb, from the south-west, in 1928.

Seat too far where the outer arm of the Cobb reaches into the waves.

That year the association was formalised between Sir Francis Walsingham (1530–90) and the town of Lyme. He obviously already knew and liked the town as he chose it in preference to Banbury. Both constituencies had elected him to the House of Commons. In Westminster he came to the attention of Sir William Cecil, the Lord Treasurer, who was impressed by the nature of Walsingham's contacts in France and Italy, and his 'exceptional dexterity in extracting information from them'.

Although he was never officially appointed, in 1559 he became 'chief organiser of the English Government's secret service in London.' He ran a network of agents including Lyme's own Arthur Gregory. Walsingham, personally, proved pivotal in breaking an international conspiracy organised by Florentine merchant Roberto di Ridolfi. The plot was aimed at assassinating Queen Elizabeth, following which there was to be an uprising to restore Catholicism, with Mary Queen of Scots marrying the Duke of Norfolk and being placed on the throne.

Arthur Gregory died in retirement in Lyme in 1605. Whether or not it was known in the town, he was one of the first practitioners of a surreptitious science, and he remains one of the great names in the annals of the secret intelligence service. Gregory had the 'admirable art', historian Thomas Fuller (1608–61) of Broadwindsor recorded, 'of forcing the seal of a letter, yet so invisibly that it still appeared a virgin to the exact beholder.' Walsingham, Fuller wrote, made considerable use of him to intercept the 'pacquet' – the diplomatic bag – 'which passed from foreign parts to Mary, Queen of Scotland.' He was rewarded with a pension from the Exchequer. These interceptions remained sensitive for centuries. Postal communications monitored in 1794, for example, were not declassified until 1995.

Walsingham represented Lyme Regis until 1567 and was the English ambassador in Paris from 1570. There he saved a young Philip Sidney from the St Bartholomew's Day massacre of Protestants on 24 August 1572. Back in Lyme Regis there were also primitive religious differences. The bizarre state of both popular beliefs and the legal system is shown by a Lyme case in which widow Johanna Ellesdon declared upon oath, in 1569, that her neighbour Ellen Walker was 'a witch' who had been seen to vomit pins and needles. Such were the grass-roots issues of domestic life. Returning to Britain, to become Queen Elizabeth's joint Secretary of State on 20 December 1573, Walsingham resumed his place in the House of Commons as county member for Surrey and retained the seat for life.

Lyme's townsmen were more concerned with commercial realities than witchcraft and discussed ways of protecting their wealth from outrages by man and nature. The former could be countered by ordnance, powder and shot. The latter required great piles to withstand 'the violence and fretting of the sea'. They also felt the need to be protected from the intemperate behaviour of one another. A bylaw was passed by the borough, in 1570, requiring that discussions were not to be conducted with vehemence or indecent words. The penalty for infringement was substantial, being a 40-shilling fine, payable on the Cobb.

In anticipation of the threat of a gathering Spanish Armada, coastal features around Lyme Regis were surveyed in 1586 and the plan placed in Queen Elizabeth's library. The Cobb was regarded as a likely invasion target. Sixty troops were posted to prepare defences to repel landing parties. The port was also required to fit out two ships, the 60-ton *Revenge* and 90-ton *Jacob*, as its contribution to the Royal Navy. In the event the enemy fleet passed by, en route to the Netherlands where it was tasked to pick up the Spanish army, and was thwarted by a combination of English harassment, misjudgement, and our old friend the weather.

On Sunday 21 July 1588, Don Miguele de Oquendo's flagship *San Salvador*, carrying the paymaster and treasure chests of the Spanish Armada, lost much of her stern and superstructure in an explosion off the Devon coast. She was partially emptied by the enemy and then abandoned, to drift across Lyme Bay with injured crew still on board, off the Chesil Beach. Captain Flemyng, in the pinnace *Golden Hind*, secured her with a line and towed her around Portland Bill into Portland Roads, the anchorage off Weymouth. She was emptied there and considered sufficiently seaworthy to be towed to Portsmouth but keeled over and sank in Studland Bay.

Bree's maritime survey of 1589 names Lyme Regis as the third-largest port in England. London had six times as many ships, and Bristol came a reasonable second, but Lyme still led all the other lesser ports. The Devon mariner Sir Walter Raleigh was a regular visitor, calling on his Cobham family friends at Colway Manor.

Sir Richard Grenville, in the Lyme vessel *Revenge*, operated with the Azores Fleet of Lord Thomas Howard in 1591. Whilst intercepting Spanish treasure ships returning from America, Grenville found himself isolated from the remainder of the English vessels, off Flores. The *Revenge* fought alone against 15 Spanish ships but Sir Richard refused to surrender. He died of his wounds; although many of the crew survived.

As a result, in recognition of the contribution that the 'ancient and populous borough' had made during these troubled times, Queen Elizabeth confirmed Lyme's royal charter, in the hope that it would 'for ever remain a town of peace and quietness to the fear and terror of evil men.'

Chapter 3

SOMERS, BERMUDA & THE TEMPEST

It was an age of discovery. Bags of gold-dust and stacks of elephant ivory arrived in Lyme, after the *Cherubim* discovered Senegal and the Gambia in 1591, although it was not until 1723 that Captain Stubbs sailed up the great West African river. England's south-western ports throbbed with travellers' tales of fantastic places, fearsome sea creatures, and the anthropology of race. Most of the planet was uncharted and much of the land beyond visited shores was also unknown.

Sir George Somers (1554–1610), a retired buccaneer and veteran of three voyages to the Azores, was knighted by King James I at Whitehall on 23 July 1603. He returned to his west-Dorset home, Berne Farm at Whitchurch Canonicorum in the coastal hinterland of Charmouth, which he had bought in 1587. He was well known at Lyme, only three miles away, as it was his local port. Sir George was their sort of man, as they proved on 25 February 1604 by electing him as the member of Parliament for Lyme Regis.

On 23 May 1609, King James appointed Sir George as Admiral of the Association of the South Virginian Company. Retirement over, he fitted out a fleet of nine ships to convey a fresh band of colonists across the Atlantic Ocean to Jamestown, which was troubled by native unrest and a want of food and supplies.

The next news to reach England, in 1610, was that the expedition for the relief of the Virginia colony was scattered by a hurricane when it was eight weeks out in the mid-Atlantic. The commander of the fleet, Sir George Somers in *Sea Venture*, was

NOVA BRITANNIA.

OFFERING MOST

Excellent fruites by Planting in
VIRGINIA.

Exciting all such as be well affected
to further the same.

LONDON
Printed for SAMVEL MACHAM, and are to be sold at
his Shop in Pauls Church-yard, at the
Signe of the Bul-head.
1609.

'Nova Britannia' was across the sea in Virginia, but en route Sir George Somers founded Bermuda.

wrecked on the rocks of the islands known as the Bermudas from the Spaniard, Juan Bermuda, who first sighted them in 1515. There, on 25 July 1609, Sir George's crew found their salvation with abundant food in the form of easily caught shoals of fish, turtles, hogs, fowl, eggs and edible fruit. There was also timber, which enabled them to build two ships, *Patience* and *Providence*, in which they sailed again for Virginia, on 10 May 1610. Meanwhile, the possession of the Bermudas, which were now to be known as Virginiola, was established in the name of King James. Sir George left a group of men there to ensure continuance of the British claim.

Then on 23 May 1610 the salvation of Jamestown and its distressed Virginian colonists was achieved, with the arrival of the vessels from Bermuda. They were followed, two weeks later, by Thomas West and another relief party from England. Meanwhile, the adventures of Sir George Somers and the *Sea Venture* were being recorded by another Lyme man, Silvester Jourdain, who was accompanying his townsman and penning *A Discovery of the Bermudas, otherwise called the Isle of Devils*. A copy found its way into the hands of playwright William Shakespeare who was inspired to begin work on *The Tempest*.

Most Lyme boys dreamed of going off to sea, and many found the opportunity of doing so; Silvester Jourdain was spurred into acting out his dream after a rebuff by the borough council. As a result of a 'contumacious' spat at a meeting in 1598 he was ordered to remain behind afterwards, alone in the building, for five hours as a punishment. Instead he walked home and turned his back on Lyme, having forfeited his status as a freeman, and found himself in a position to tell the world about the creation of one of the first and last of British colonial possessions.

The twist in the tail of what had shaped up into a great story was that Sir George Somers died in the Bermudas on 9 November 1610 from what was described as 'a surfeit of eating a pig'. His heart was buried there, at St George, Bermuda, beneath a wooden cross, but the body was embalmed for return to England. His nephew, Matthew Somers, returned with it to Britain for a burial with military honours in the Parish Church at Whitchurch Canonicorum.

Then, on 19 June 1611, Matthew Somers set sail back to the islands of the Bermudas with a supply of fish and hogs for onward transit to the hunger-stricken colonists of Jamestown, Virginia.

As a tribute to the town, the Royal Navy named the first warship to carry the name of the borough, HMS *Lyme Regis*, which won battle honours in 1657 at Seaton Cruz and was still in service a century later when she fought at Lagos Bay, Portugal, on 17–18 August 1759. Admiral Edward Boscawen took on the Toulon fleet under French Admiral de la Clue who lost both his legs in the engagement and died the following day. Four French vessels were lost and the remainder ran for safety in Cadiz.

Lyme seaman Sir George Somers and his globe.

The lodestone with which George Somers magnetised his compass.

Left: *Tempest Cottage, above Fishpond Bottom, was the home of Lyme mariner Silvester Jourdain who brought home the story of the Bermuda discovery by shipwreck which William Shakespeare turned into a play.*

Staff list of the Customs House at Lyme, employing 11 officers, tidesmen and boatmen (centre), in 1671.

Saturday Magazine.

Nº 51.　　　APRIL 20ᵀᴴ, 1833　　　{ PRICE ONE PENNY.

UNDER THE DIRECTION OF THE COMMITTEE OF GENERAL LITERATURE AND EDUCATION,
APPOINTED BY THE SOCIETY FOR PROMOTING CHRISTIAN KNOWLEDGE.

NATIONAL STATUES.

STATUE OF KING CHARLES THE FIRST, AT CHARING CROSS.

VOL. II.　　　　　　　　　　　　　51

King Charles I, seen on his equestrian statue at Charing Cross, ordered the siege of republican Lyme.

Chapter 4

CIVIL WAR SIEGE

In 1981 I acquired and donated to the town's Philpot Museum the earliest document relating to the Civil War siege of the town. With the help of the museum's curator, the novelist John Fowles, I researched the background to Charles I's signed command for 'forces to be sent against Lyme'. It is dated 11 February 1644 – shown as 1643 on the document as this was before the calendar change of 1751, which moved the year's legal end from 31 March to 31 December – and addressed from the King's court at Oxford: 'To our trusty and wellbeloved Sir John Stawell, Knight of the Bath and Governor of Taunton.'

Sir John Stawell (1599–1662) was appointed Royalist Governor at Taunton Castle in June 1643. The impression of the royal seal of England is on the rear side, right, towards the foot of the page. The wax of the seal has dried and detached itself from the paper. Lyme in 1644 was still one of the most important ports in England. Its significance during the dispute between King Charles and Parliament lay in its position, strategically placed at the approaches to the south-western peninsula. Puritans had already become the dominant section of the population, having displayed their power by abolishing the age-old Cobb Ale festivities which were celebrated at Whitsun. But at the time the letter was written, and despite the successes on land in 1643, the main military weakness of the Royalist cause lay in their inability to control the sea.

Taking Lyme by land therefore became a major test case for the Royalists. Resistance was equally important from the Parliamentary point of view. The letter deals with the preparations for the attack. Previously, in 1642, Sir John Stawell had raised three regiments of horse and two regiments of foot, at his own expense. His instructions in 1644 read:

Whereas we understand ye condition of ye rebellious town of Lyme to be such, as (by God's blessing) ye present addition of some few more foot forces may bring the same into our submission and obedience; we have therefore thought fit to require you forthwith to send 200 of your foot together with their arms and pay, to that work (the like whereof we have ordered Colonel Wyndham to do also) to be returned back again to you at the end of that service, which we conceive and hope will be speedily. And hereof we desire you by no means to fail. And this

Our Letter shall be your Warrant on that behalf. Given at Our Court at Oxford ye 11th day of February 1643. By his Majesty's Command. Edward Nicholas.

Sir Edward Nicholas (1593–1669), knighted on 26 November 1641, became Secretary of State to the King at the end of that year. The Oxford headquarters of his secretariat were at Pembroke College. Colonel Wyndham proved more difficult to identify as several Wyndhams were active in the Royalist cause. The choice here lay between George, Francis and Edmund, all of whom were colonels. George, however, was a Parliamentary prisoner at Poole at this date. Colonel Francis Wyndham was in Somerset as Governor of Dunster Castle. Colonel Edmund Wyndham was also in Somerset as Governor of Bridgwater Castle. The latter seemed favourite but there was also a Colonel John Wyndham who the antiquary and biographer John Aubrey says was 'in charge of the King's garrison at Salisbury'.

The Royalist forces led by Prince Maurice of the Rhine duly besieged the Cromwellian town of Lyme Regis in an episode that began to bite on 20 April 1644. He established his headquarters in the Alford family home at Haye House, on the north side of Haye Lane, and gathered his forces around nearby Colway Manor. His army of 6,000 men were pitted against the 4,000 inhabitants of Lyme. Probably less than 1,000 of these were trained soldiers, while many of the rest were women, children or too old to be of much help. Yet in terms of commanding officers, John Fowles points out that 'the odds were all on Lyme's side'. Their garrison commander was Robert Blake, later Admiral Blake, 'one of the shrewdest military minds of the entire period.'

There were fields between the Roman Road and Colway Lane and the battle lines on the edge of town. The Royalists failed to take their primary objective, the Cobb harbour, which at this time was a detached quay separated from the adjacent mainland by an area of foreshore. Morale in the town was lifted in spirit by a reputed total of 23 Puritan preachers, given the practical boost of successful skirmishes on land, and reinforced by supply runs by sea. By 28 May 1644 it was clear that despite the town's discomfort, Prince Maurice no longer had time on his side, as the King wrote in another letter:

As soon as you shall have finished what can be done upon Lyme, or shall plainly see that it is not to be taken; we desire you to draw with all your forces to Bristol.

Despite that order, and stalemate on the ground, Prince Maurice kept the siege going for another ineffectual month. The town's fleet of boats continued to break the land blockade and thatch was stripped from roofs to reduce the danger from flaming arrows that rained down on the town from the attackers on the hill. Exchanges of musket-fire from either side of the earthwork defences to the town amounted to little more than mutual harassment, although an evening raid accounted for Lyme's most effective defender. Captain Pyne commanded its cavalry regiment and had for a year taken the Civil War into the Royalist camp with repeated sallies against their positions. The other heroes were the town's determined womenfolk who dressed as soldiers to give an impression of greater numbers and sustained the resistance. This produced an epic of the conflict versified to establish a morale-boosting legend for Puritan London. Revd James Strong, the rector of Bettiscombe in the hills beyond Marshwood Vale, wrote *Joanereidos*, which carries the following explanatory sub-title:

Feminine valour: eminently discovered in Western women: as well as by defying the merciless enemy at the face abroad, as by fighting against them in the Garrison towns, sometimes carrying stones, anon tumbling of stones over the Works on the enemy, when they have been scaling them, some carrying powder, others charging pieces to ease the soldiers, constantly resolved for generality, not to think any one's life dear, to maintain that Christian quarrel for the Parliament. Whereby, as they deserve commendations in themselves, so are they prepared as example unto others.

Eight weeks of siege ended on 16 June 1644 when Prince Maurice finally came to terms with reality. It was claimed that he lost 'between 2,000 to 3,000 men in the attacks'. This was certainly greatly exaggerated, but even the Royalists admitted their Lyme casualties were higher than those they suffered at either Exeter or Bristol. Parliamentary losses of the defenders were relatively light, being given as 120, although there was damage of one kind or another to almost every building in the town.

Lyme also almost played a part in the final act of the Civil War. After the execution of his father, defeated at the Battle of Worcester, where he fled from the vicinity of St Martin's Gate, Worcester, on the evening of 3 September 1651, vanquished 21-year-old monarch Charles II embarked on one of history's great escapes. It saw him disguised as a woman and a servant and hiding in an oak tree – spawning a forest of Royal Oak pub names – and secreted in priest holes, such as that provided by

Colonel Francis Wyndham in Trent Manor on the borders of Somerset and Dorset. He carried a reward of £1,000 on his head for 'a tall man, above two yards high, with dark brown hair scarcely distinguished from black.' The King himself told the story to diarist Samuel Pepys nearly three decades later.

He had arrived at Trent from Castle Cary Manor, Somerset, where he was sheltered by Edward Kyton, steward to the Marquis of Hertford. The Trent household was headed by Francis and Anne Wyndham and included Anne's cousin by marriage, Juliana Coningsby, and her sister, Mrs Elizabeth Reymes. Elizabeth's husband, Bullen, was the Royalist squire Bullayne Reymes. Francis' elder brother, Colonel Edmund Wyndham, was married to the King's nurse, Christabel Pyne. Francis had served under the King's companion, Lord Wilmot, and held Dunster Castle for the King's father in the Civil War. They had impeccable Royalist credentials but Francis and Anne had only recently moved to Trent.

This might have compromised the situation but the Wyndhams had inherited reliable local knowledge from taking on former Gerard family retainer Henry Rogers. He warned them 'to avoid the jealous eyes of some neighbours' named Young. Otherwise, Trent was and is a quiet place, and the Manor House hiding hole is dated from the days when it was owned by recusants.

The King, dressed in 'a kind of grey cloth suit', was pretending to be the servant of Jane Lane. She rode pillion to him on arrival. It was mid-morning on 17 September 1651. Anne Wyndham, in particular, was overcome by emotion on receiving 'so glorious a prince thus eclipsed'. Thomas Blount, a Catholic lawyer, records that she paid him 'the homage of tears'.

Francis Wyndham visited Sir John Strangways and his sons at Melbury House, hoping that as the family estate included the Abbotsbury coast they could arrange a boat to France, but Sir John was reluctant to become directly involved. He did, however, provide £100 to finance the operation. Bullen Reymes had already arranged for Captain William Ellesdon of Lyme Regis to take Sir John Berkeley to France. It was decided to use Ellesdon again. He duly made the arrangements for the party to join the next boat due to leave Lyme for France, which was skippered by Stephen Limbry, who rented his home from Ellesdon. The crew were told that they were picking up a Mr Payne, a bankrupt merchant who was escaping from his creditors, with a servant.

The party comprised the King, Juliana Coningsby, Francis Wyndham and servant Henry Peters, and Henry, Lord Wilmot (later Lord Rochester, 1612–58), who refused to disguise himself, apart from carrying a hawk on his wrist so he looked like a hunting gentleman. He was bulky and brave, the cavalry leader who swept to victory on Roundway Down, near Devizes. Wilmot was Groom of the Bedchamber when King Charles I went to his execution at the Banqueting Hall in Whitehall. 'I could never get him to put on any disguises – he saying he should look frightfully in it,' the King told Pepys. They crossed west Dorset, via Broadwindsor, to the home of Ellesdon's brother at Monkton Wyld in the hills above Lyme where they were met by Ellesdon. He confirmed the arrangements. The main party were to stay at the Queen's Arms in Charmouth that night, 22 September, while Wyndham and Peters kept lookout on Charmouth beach for the approach of Limbry's ship.

Limbry was promised £60 upon landing them at St Malo. The group prepared for an early leave and Wyndham and Peters stayed on the beach to await the boat, but none arrived. Fearful of arousing suspicions, by waiting about in daylight, they decided to abort the plan and head eastwards. The absence of the boat is said to have been caused by Limbry's wife, concerned that Stephen might end up with a rope around his neck, having locked him in the bedroom and hidden his trousers for good measure.

Dangers to the royal party progressed from bad to worse. They were almost captured by troops at the (Old) George Inn in the centre of Bridport and escaped along Lee Lane at Bradpole on 23 September 1651. The event is commemorated by a rough-hewn block of Bothenhampton stone erected near its main road junction by Alexander Meyrick Broadley on the anniversary in 1901. The last landward leg of the royal route ended safely at Shoreham, on boarding the *Surprise*, which took the King to exile in France.

Prince Rupert of the Rhine, the King's Captain-General, who was commanded to capture Lyme.

Lyme's Nonconformist stance in the Civil War found its religious expression in the Baptist Chapel beside the junction of Silver Street and Sherborne Lane in 1653. Silver Street takes its name from the Latin word 'silva' for trees, as a reference to its once-wooded setting, rather than being a reference to the metal. The Congregational Chapel in Coombe Street was founded in 1662.

Lyme as a port received something of a war-dividend from seventeenth-century upheavals. Construction work turned the Cobb from an unattached scythe-shaped single wall – cut off at high tide by a channel at the western extremity, to enable the ebb and flow of shingle – into a triple-branched shape (although the western channel remained open to reduce 'storm-pressures' on the High Wall). The South Wall of the Cobb, extending eastwards from the High Wall into Lyme Bay, was the defiant addition to act as a protective breakwater for the main quay. Likewise, the detached North Wall, across the entry channel, which joins the mainland on the south-west side of Cobb Gate Beach.

Structurally and literally, the Cobb still stood alone, as the figurative high-water mark of Lyme as a port. Customs takings here in 1677 were still in excess of those from Liverpool. In the 1680s it ranked fourteenth in the whole country and in Dorset terms it was second only to Poole, although the combined activity of Melcombe Regis and Weymouth were greater. It is therefore not that surprising that Lyme should have been in the mind of exiled conspirators as they contemplated high treason.

Charles R.

Trusty & welbeloved Wee greete you well. Whereas Wee understand ye Condicón of ye rebellious Towne of Lyme to be such, as (by Gods blessing) ye present addicón of some few more foote forces may bring the same into Our subiecón & obedience; Wee haue therefore thought fitt to require you forthwith to send twoe hundred of yor foote togethir with their Armes & Pay, to that Work (the like whereof Wee haue ordered Col. Wyndham to doe also) to be returned back againe to you at the end of that Service, wch Wee conceiue & hope wilbe speedily. And herein Wee desire you by noe meanes to faile: And these Our Letters shalbe yor Warrant in that behalfe. Given at Our Court at Oxford ye 11th day of february 1643.

By his Matie Command

Edw Nicholas

The King's order for the Lyme seige, signed on 11 February 1643
(which became 1644 after the calendar change).

THE
SOULDIERS
CATECHISME:

Compofed for
The Parliaments Army:

Confifting of two Parts : wherein
are chiefly taught :

1 *The Iuftification* } of our Souldiers.
2 *The Qualification*

Written for the Incouragement and In-
ftruction of all that have taken up Armes in
this Caufe of God and his People; efpe-
cially the common Souldiers.

2 Sam. 10.12. *Be of good courage, and let us
play the men for our people, and for the Ci-
ties of our God, and the Lord do that which
feemeth him good.*

Deut. 23.9. *When the Hoft goeth forth againft
thine enemies, then keepe thee from every
wicked thing.*

Imprimatur. JA. CRANFORD.

Printed for J. Wright *in the Old-Baily.* 1644

Qualms about a just war, answered by
Robert Ram, winning God's support
for the Parliamentary side.

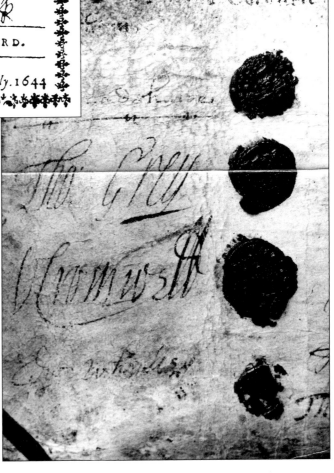

*Final solution – Oliver Cromwell's
signature on the death warrant
of Charles I.*

41

Charismatic and handsome James Scott, Duke of Monmouth, whose invasion at Lyme in July 1685 put him into the dustbin of history.

Monmouth wearing the 'George' badge of the Order of the Garter, depicting Saint George (himself) slaying the dragon (King James II).

Chapter 5

MONMOUTH'S REIGN & JEFFREYS' REVENGE

*In Pinhay Bay, out of sight from Lyme, the rebel
Duke's ships hid as he prepared to land.*

The town originally chosen to provide a means of escape for a fugitive monarch was selected by Lucy Walter, Monmouth's mother, as the point of arrival for the late King's handsome illegitimate son, on his way to claim the Stuart crown from his uncle, King James II. Once again the secret was maintained until the ship carrying James Scott, Duke of Monmouth, anchored offshore on Thursday 11 June 1685. He had been smuggled aboard at Santford, in the Netherlands, wearing 'seaman's apparel and with great whiskers'.

The Mayor, George Alford, Samuel Dassell and the burgesses of Lyme were playing bowls, Drake-like on a green to the south of Pound Street, as the invaders approached. From here they overlooked the Cobb, at the bottom of Stile Lane, and carried on play as two unidentified vessels came inshore from due south, far out across Lyme Bay. Unusually, the ships anchored in Pinhay Bay, behind Devonshire Head and Seven Rock Point to the west of the Cobb, where they were beyond the arc of fire of the town's cannon.

The responsibility for checking them was delegated to the borough surveyor who was sent out in a rowing-boat. To the alarm of the town, he did not return, and the bell was rung on Bell Cliff. The order was given to prepare the guns in the forts there and on the Cobb but no powder could be found. Anxieties increased as the vessels were joined by a third Dutch vessel which had anchored four miles to the east during the morning, to enable two men to be rowed ashore at Seatown beach in the parish of Chideock. An Englishman, Thomas Dare, was accompanied by Andrew, Lord Fletcher, a fiery Scot. The latter was the second-in-command of exiled Protestant Duke of Monmouth's rebel cavalry. They were tasked to make their way inland, to Forde Abbey, to liaise with landowning sympathisers.

Meanwhile, that evening, the Western Rebellion began, as the Duke of Monmouth landed with 82 of his men. They came ashore from the 32-gun Dutch frigate *Helderenburg* on the pebble beach in Poker's Pool –

The George Inn in Coombe Street, where Monmouth gathered his rebels, was destroyed by fire on 11 May 1844.

since known as Monmouth Beach – to the west of the Cobb harbour at Lyme Regis, and unfurled a green banner with gold embroidered lettering: 'Fear nothing but God.' Monmouth knelt on the beach and kissed a pebble. The party set off up the Stile Path to meet the townspeople. Monmouth made his headquarters the (Old) George Inn, in Coombe Street, which was a rambling building that burnt down on 11 May 1844. The Duke's own unit was the Red Regiment under Lieutenant-Colonel Thomas Wade and Major Nathaniel Wade. Monmouth split his forces into three companies. Two were to guard 'the avenues of the town' while the third, under Major Wade, prepared to unload and mount four cannon. These artillery pieces were successfully landed overnight, thanks to willing hands from Lyme's mariners, and the co-operation of Lyme's 'Cromwellian townspeople'.

On 13 June the plan started to unravel. The Duke of Monmouth's advance party bungled its task, after leaving Forde Abbey to join the main force at Lyme Regis. Thomas Dare had successfully commandeered 40 horses and well-armed men at Forde Abbey, but Andrew Fletcher pulled rank in a dispute as to who should ride the best horse. The Englishman refused to relinquish his prize and raised his whip in defiance. Fletcher lifted his gun and shot Dare through the head.

Volunteers who witnessed the incident wanted Fletcher strung up for murder but he was smuggled back onto his ship and would escape in the *Helderenburg* to Spain. This disastrous own goal deprived Monmouth of two key players. Fletcher could have been invaluable as an aggressive Scot was just what Monmouth lacked at the head of his cavalry for a forthcoming skirmish at Bridport and the decisive rout at the Battle of Sedgemoor. Instead he was saddled with the hapless Lord Grey. Thomas Dare had also been a valuable asset, proving himself capable of winning confidence from the local gentry and populace, and vital for success as paymaster for the operation. This element of the plot caused immediate problems and Monmouth seized £400 from the Customs House in Lyme. He left a signed receipt for the 'loan'. Others failed to match Dare's practical ability at finding horses and despite searching the countryside they remained in short supply throughout the campaign.

King James II's forces were alerted to events in Lyme by George Alford, from one of its few staunch Royalist families, at Haye House. The first military

The early-sixteenth-century Old Monmouth Hotel, on the corner of Church Street and Monmouth Street, where Lord Grey based himself.

THE DUKE OF MONMOUTH AT LYME REGIS. 1685.

THIS SCENE REPRESENTS A PORTION OF THE WALL DECORATION OF THE OLD TIME DORSET EXHIBITION AT WIMBORNE

THE EXHIBITION ARTIST IS INDEBTED TO LOCAL GENTLEMEN WHO KINDLY FURNISHED SOME DETAILS OF THE MONMOUTH RISING. THE YOUNG DUKE IS SEEN HOLDING HIS STANDARD, SUPPORTED BY AN OTHER ADVENTUROUS SPIRIT LORD GREY; WHILE FERGUSSON MAKES OUT THE FATAL ROLL UPON WHICH MANY A POOR RECRUIT HAD REASON TO WISH HIS NAME HAD NEVER APPEARED.

Monmouth and his standard hoping to change history, with Lord Grey (right), as Fergusson enrolls another inadequately qualified recruit.

THE MONMOUTH RISING   LYME REGIS 1685.

SCENE FORMING PART OF THE WALL DECORATIONS OF THE OLD TIME DORSET
EXHIBITION AT WIMBORNE   WILD ENTHUSIASM FOR THE PURITAN CAUSE
MARKED THE MORNING FOLLOWING THE LANDING OF THE DUKES LITTLE PARTY
OF ADVENTURERS   BUT THE EYE OF THE TRAINED SOLDIER WOULD HAVE MARK-
ED THE ABSENCE OF MATERIAL SUITABLE FOR WARFARE.   HORSES STRAIGHT
FROM THE PLOUGH   PITCHFORKS AND SYTHES, WERE FOREDOOMED AGAINST
THE TROOPERS OF THE KING AT SEDGEMOOR

*Puritan exuberance backed by pitchforks and scythes as the cause
of the Duke of Monmouth stirs Lyme into action.*

exchange of the uprising took place on 14 June. Colonel Thomas Venner led the Red Regiment of rebel cavalry eastwards to Bridport where they thought they could soon overcome the Constable's watchmen and gather armed defectors for the rebel cause. Unknown to them, the Dorset Militia had arrived and based themselves in the Bull, in East Street. Venner's men came under gunfire from windows at the hostelry. Monmouth's men stormed the building and broke down its doors, but several lives were lost in the process. They included, on the King's side, Dorset gentlemen Edward Coker of Mappowder and Wadham Strangways of Abbotsbury, both of whom were killed by Colonel Venner. Two of the King's men did manage to escape. One hid in an attic and the other lay low in a plot of kidney beans. As he searched for them, a shot from the dark wounded Colonel Venner in the stomach, following which he gave the order to retreat. Lord Grey's supporting horsemen also bolted, westwards to Charmouth, at the sound of gunfire. Major Nathaniel Wade restored discipline and prepared to hold the bridge over the River Brit with his foot-soldiers, but the Dorset Militia contented themselves with an arms-length exchange of insults. Eastwards, the town itself across to the other bridge over the River Asker was held for the King.

Offshore, there was a further debacle, as Captain Trevenion in HMS *Saudadoes* captured the two smaller Dutch vessels in Lyme Bay. One was a flat-bottomed pink and the other a two-masted dogger. These fishing smacks gave their name to the Dogger Bank. It might not have mattered much if they had been unloaded, but Captain Trevenion found himself in possession of 40 barrels of gunpowder and a mass of salted meat, comprising 'backs, breasts and pots', estimated to be sufficient to feed an army of thousands. Monmouth now found himself desperately short of all resources in six out of the seven categories of military necessities – expertise, manpower, munitions, transport, food and money. I include as the seventh the element of surprise. This was still his to exploit but it was destined to join the others.

Hotel life and times, including Monmouth rebels, Oscar Wilde, and the British Army.

A similar mixture of indecision and failure continued until the fateful day on 'sad Sedgemoor' in the Somerset Levels. Having left Lyme at the head of 3,000 men, to occupy Taunton and Bridgwater, the Duke balked at the chance of taking what might well have been a willing Bristol, and went back to a dismal defeat in the middle of nowhere. One final mistake sealed his fate.

'Beware of the rhyne,' the Duke is said to have been warned, but despite thinking of the river in Germany he must have been aware of them already. No one who has walked across the Somerset Levels – let alone led a peasant army around them in ever-decreasing circles – could be unaware of these little local difficulties. Deep drainage channels, known as rhynes, make the peaty flatlands an impossible place in which to manoeuvre.

So, on Monday 6 July 1685, his rebels paid the price. They were routed in what was to be the last battle fought on English soil. Those not slain on the spot or strung up in the immediate aftermath took their chances of hanging or transportation, to the Caribbean colonies, before Judge Jeffreys' Bloody Assize. Monmouth escaped as far as Horton Heath in Dorset but was captured, taken to the Tower of London, and beheaded by his uncle. His execution was hardly clean-cut, but it was dignified and humane compared with the hideous end of the hundreds condemned by Lord Chief Justice George Jeffreys.

His revenge and retribution on Lyme Regis took place on Saturday 12 September 1685. Because of its symbolism, as the starting-point for the shambolic Western Rebellion, a dozen representative victims were chosen to be hanged, drawn and quartered on the Monmouth Beach landing-place of the unfortunate Duke. It was observed by Mr Pitts, a spectator, that they were to have been drawn to the place of execution by a sledge, but that no cart-horses, or even coach-horses, could be made to draw it, so they were obliged to go on foot. This was much remarked at the time, and was considered by many as a kind of miracle. Each was to be fully disembowelled and butchered. Their body parts were dipped in tar

Monmouth House in Monmouth Street keeps the memory alive but was rebuilt a century later.

Monmouth Beach, west of the Cobb, where Monmouth landed and his adherents paid the price.

Lyme's villain is George Jeffreys, Lord Chief Justice, whose retribution for the Monmouth Rebellion included 12 gruesome executions on the beach west of the Cobb.

and distributed for display across the affected counties as a gruesome warning of the price for treason. Those who succumbed to this fate were as follows:

1. Lieutenant-Colonel Abraham Holmes, an old and gallant officer, who had served under Cromwell with distinction. He accompanied the Duke to Holland, and was made a Major-General by him. In the action at Norton St Philip, Somerset:

> *... one of his arms was shot to pieces so that it hung only by the flesh; and in consequence of this being soon taken, was stripped by the soldiers and carried naked before a Justice of the Peace who humanely clothed him. His shattered arm being an encumbrance to him, he laid it on a dresser and cut it off himself with the cook-maid's knife. He was hanged on the very spot where he landed with the Duke.*

2. Christopher Battiscombe was a young gentleman, who lived near Lyme.

> *He was several times at the Judge's lodgings, who offered him pardon if he would impeach others, which he nobly refused. Among the petitioners for his life was a young lady to whom he was engaged to be married; who [made] her humble request on her knees to the Judge.*

She is said to have received this reply:

> *That he could only spare her part of him; but as he knew what she wanted, it should be that part which she liked best, and he would give orders to the sheriff accordingly.*

3. Lieutenant William Hewling, but 20 years old, whose brother Benjamin suffered similarly at Taunton. They were fashionable Londoners, related to Cromwell. The maidens of Lyme, partly by the assistance of the populace and also by connivance of the persons in power, would recover William's remains for burial in Lyme churchyard.

4. Sampson Larke, a learned and pious Dissenting teacher of Lyme, who was about to make a speech, but was interrupted by the guard with the laconic observation that the work of the day being so great, they could not afford him time.

5. Dr Benjamin Temple, from Nottingham, was the Duke's physician in Holland, and knew nothing about the intention of invading England until they were at sea.

6. Captain Arthur Matthews, who died very heroically, forgiving the executioner but advising him to leave off his bloody trade. The hangman replied 'that he was forced to do it against his mind.'

7. Joseph Tyler, a learned Bristol gentleman, who had a command in the Duke's army. He wrote a hymn shortly before he was to die.

8. William Cox, who was the first man to enlist with the Duke after his landing and whose two sons, John and Philip, were are also condemned (although they would be reprieved and transported to the West Indies).

9. Samuel Robins, a Charmouth fisherman, who boarded the Duke's ship to sell his catch. He was then compelled to pilot the vessel into Lyme. Judge Jeffreys would have pardoned him, but for it being proved in court that a subversive book, entitled *The Solemn League and Covenant*, had been found in his house.

10. Josias Ascue, about whom nothing is known.

11. John Madders, Constable of Crewkerne, forwarded news of the Duke's landing to King James II, but then accepted command of a company in Monmouth's service and would be taken prisoner at the Battle of Sedgemoor. He might have been pardoned, but for the Lord Chief Justice hearing him described as 'a good Protestant'. Jeffreys snapped: 'Oho! He is a Presbyterian. I can smell them 40 miles. He shall be hanged.'

12. Captain John Kidd, a man of great courage, beheld the other 11 dead before him and said it was a dreadful sight. After praying devoutly for some time he seemed comforted and resigned to his fate.

John Holloway appeared in arms at Lyme Regis at the time of Monmouth's landing, in order to oppose him, but 'not being properly supported' he joined the Duke's party. He later surrendered himself in response to the King's proclamation, in order to obtain a pardon, but was a few hours late. As a result he appeared before Judge Jeffreys and was sentenced to hang, with the execution being carried out that month, in September 1685. He told his guards: 'You seem to be brave fellows; but if I were to have my life for fighting the best five of you, I should not question it.'

The same contemporary account tells us about another unfortunate Lyme resident whose plea of mitigation was turned against him:

John Bennett, a very aged man of Lyme, who was supported by the parish, and which circumstance was mentioned to Judge Jeffreys, he replied that they had no occasion to trouble themselves on that account, for he would ease them of the charge. At the place of execution, his son offered to die in his stead, and actually attempted going up the ladder for that purpose.

'The Defeat of the Rebels' at the Battle of Sedgemoor on Sunday 5 July 1685, as depicted on a contemporary playing card.

As a result, Chatham House in Broad Street at Lyme Regis – formerly called the Great House – is haunted by the ghost of Judge Jeffreys. He visited the town to see the aftermath of royal revenge. The heads of two of the victims of the Bloody Assize were impaled on the spiked iron gates of the Great House as Jeffreys dined in splendour with Mayor Alford. They ate sturgeon. The ghost of Judge Jeffreys is said to stalk the house. He wears a wig and the black cap donned for pronouncing sentence of death. The spectre brandishes a bloody bone. Such sightings are rare, however, and have only been recorded from times when the building is empty.

One of the few lucky ones who committed an indiscretion at Lyme in the summer of 1685 but went on to find fame and fortune was 24-year-old Daniel Foe who changed his name in 1703 and is known to us as the journalist and novelist Daniel Defoe (1661–1731). His part in the rebellion was never publicly explained, and he hesitated about joining the next insurgents from the West Country in 1688 until it became clear that they were going to be the winning side. He decided that this time the invasion force would have to prove its worth by crossing the Thames. There he met Prince William of Orange at Henley, to offer his services in completing the Glorious Revolution.

He was a trooper on horseback for the escort of William and Mary to a triumphal banquet in the City of London on 29 October 1689. Defoe hinted, in a pamphlet published in 1701, that he considered that Monmouth's descendants retained a claim to the succession. Perhaps wisely he never took the matter further. Other instances of political brinkmanship put him in the pillory for three days in July 1703, guarded by the people and fêted with flowers. His 'Hymn to the Pillory' saluted them:

Tell them the men that placed him here
Are scandals to the times;
Are at a loss to find his guilt,
And can't commit his crimes.

Chapter 6

CASE, CORAM, COADE & FANE

With the publication of his *Compendium Anatomicum nova methodo institutum*, in 1695, John Case of Lyme Regis became London's most famous and fashionable doctor. He followed it in 1696 with *Ars Anatomica breviter elucidata and Flos Aevi*, or *Coelestial Observations*. Then his *Angelical Guide* appeared in 1697 and the *Medical Expositer* in 1698.

Joseph Addison wrote in *The Tatler* that he had told Case that he had made more money from the distich above his door than Dryden had made from all his works:

Within this place
Lives Doctor Case.

'I thank you, good brother,' Case replied. 'Let me have all the fools, and you are heartily welcome to the rest of the practice.'

Across the West Country, parish registers recorded an exceptional gale: 'The great storm, both at sea and land, the greatest ever man knew in England was on the 26th day of November in the year 1703.' Henry Winstanley, the builder of the Eddystone Lighthouse, was swept to his death with his creation, and the Bishop of Bath and Wells and his lady were killed as the palace roof collapsed on their bed. It was estimated that a total of 8,000 people were drowned at sea and in flooded estuaries from the Severn to Holland.

Lyme at this time was becoming a centre for a prosperous industry. Lacemaking flourished around Honiton in south-east Devon and spread across the county boundary. By 1720, Lyme was a major centre of activity, and lacemaking was also a big business in Sherborne and Blandford. The latter came into vogue for high-fashion wares, costing up to £30 a yard, that were regarded as the equal of any made in Devon. In particular lace was used for steinkirks – the fashionable neckware. Hand-making of lace was a skill requiring great patience.

Apart from on horseback, the usual way of coming and going from Lyme was by sea, depending on the weather. Then in 1739 the stage-coach, introduced from France in 1580, finally made a regular appearance, although it avoided the town by taking a marginally easier route across the hills between Charmouth and Axminster via Penn Inn and Hunter's Lodge Inn. The road reaches 690 feet above sea level on Raymond's Hill and is at 590 feet beside Hunter's Lodge.

The *Exeter Flying Coach* took two days to travel down from London to Dorchester and a third day to reach Exeter. Stonebarrow Hill and the descent from Penn were the most challenging slopes of the entire journey. Neither were without their hazards, as was shown when the *Balloon* overturned in 1805 and killed Anne Pitt. The hostile terrain caused the turnpike road to be re-laid a short distance inland.

Lyme's literary associations might have been even more substantial if a visitor of 1725 had been successful in his mission. The father of the English novel, Henry Fielding (1707–54) was born at Sharpham Park, near Glastonbury, and the family moved on to Upton Grey, near Odiham, in Hampshire. Eighteen-year-old Henry left Eton and embarked on a turbulent love affair with heiress Sarah Andrews (1710–83), daughter of the late Solomon Andrews, merchant of Lyme Regis. Sarah's guardian, her uncle Andrew Tucker of Tudor House, had other ideas and wanted a marriage to his son John to keep control of the inheritance. Henry Fielding attempted to abduct her from Lyme Regis on 14 November 1725.

She was under the protection of the Chancery division of the High Court. Andrew Tucker set a servant loose on Fielding that Sunday. He was Joseph Channon who struck 'two several blows in the face and other parts of the body without any provocation.' According to Tucker, Fielding threatened retaliation in kind from his servant, Joseph Lewis, who 'will beat, wound, maim or kill him'. The Mayor, John Bowdidge, asked two constables to apprehend Fielding but Henry evaded the 'fat and greasy citizens'. He left a note for the Mayor. 'Andrew Tucker and his son John Tucker are clowns and cowards,' Fielding wrote, on a half-sheet found in Lyme's municipal records by historian Cyril Wanklyn of Overton in Charmouth Road.

John Tucker also lost the prize, however, as Sarah Andrews was packed off to Modbury in Devon where she was married to Ambrose Rhodes junr. Hence, Wanklyn points out, Rhodes found himself owning properties in Lyme for the next half century. The couple moved west, to Bellair House, Exeter, where Ambrose died in 1777. Sarah survived another

Captain Thomas Coram of Lyme Regis and Massachusetts has his statue in London, beside the children's hospital he founded, in Brunswick Square.

six years, by which time she had outlived Henry Fielding by 29 years.

Unlike John Tucker, another contemporary from Lyme paid particular attention to giving away money, rather than scheming to acquire more. Thomas Coram (1668–1751), the son of a Lyme Regis mariner, emigrated to Massachusetts in 1694 and became a shipbuilder. He retained his links with the home country and built up a fortune which enabled him to become one of the great philanthropists. In 1741 he funded the establishment of The Foundling Hospital in Hatton Garden, London, as the first institution in the capital to care for abandoned children. One of its first trustees, known as governors, was the caricaturist William Hogarth, whose resoundingly strong portrait painting of Coram is one of the best of its genre.

The Thomas Coram Foundation survives and there is an impressive statue to him in Brunswick Square, London WC1. A nearby playground has a notice saying that adults may only enter if escorted by a child. Coram had lived for some time in Taunton and gave his land there to a school. In America he launched a project for the education of indigenous Indian girls. Having dispersed his entire wealth to good causes he died a pauper, in London, at the age of 83. His example was in the mind of American philanthropist Andrew Carnegie when he declared that 'a man who dies rich dies disgraced'.

Coram is commemorated in Lyme by Coram Avenue and Coram Court. The latter overlooks the Cobb cliffs from the north side of the Holm Bush car park. Built as the Vicarage, in 1861, it was regarded as overly large and ostentatious. The Ecclesiastical Commissioners took advantage of an interregnum, in January 1887, to sell it to St Michael's College for the training of the sons of Exeter and Salisbury diocesan clergy. Revd Arthur Sharpe was the headmaster and there were 35 pupils. The Holiday Fellowship followed, naming it Coram Court, although the local name of Coram Tower suits the Scottish baronial-style architecture of George Vialls.

One of the earliest mentions of the Coade family in a Lyme Regis context dates from the middle of the eighteenth century. The *Reine Gabrielle*, laden with more than 5,000 gallons of honey from Dunkirk, was beached by a storm at Bridport on 25 March 1751. Robert Fowler Coade, a Lyme Regis merchant, organised its floating and brought the ship into the harbour at West Bay. All hands and cargo were saved:

... and re-shipped entire, without the least embezzlement from the country people, tho' they came down in large numbers to the beach the night the vessel was stranded in hopes of making a prey of both ship and cargo.

That year Warren Lisle (1699–1788), the commander of a squadron of Excise cutters engaged in the harassment of smugglers, found influential friends in the Fane family of Lyme Regis – the Earls of Westmorland – who rewarded his interest with an appointment that was in their patronage. He was declared Mayor of the town and served three terms, 1751–52, 1753–54, and during the early 1760s.

Smugglers and highwaymen were part of daily life when Anna Coade travelled down from London to Dorchester and wrote to her family in Lyme Regis on 4 December 1751:

I bless God I had a very safe journey, and though met with a Highwayman, yet a kind providence preserved us from being robbed. I caught a great cold on the road, and this air is very sharp at this time of year, which has confined me, ever since I came down, but live in hopes of being better. All friends at Dewlish are well, Mr Cousin Skinner is there. I have not yet been able to get out to pay them a visit, and the roads are too bad for them to travel far; [I] have the pleasure of hearing from [them] twice a week. I am at Mr Jacobs still, not being able to get a house at present.

The rest of the letter is taken up with religious verses for a Mr Newman, and 'a short meditation against the fears of death'. There is also an enquiry about the Lyme Regis appointment of 'a minister at Silver Street, [where] there is one Mr Spencer' she chooses to hear preach, 'who was brought up under Dr Merriott. I hear he is a serious moderate gentleman.'

Silver Street has a Baptist chapel. Anna Coade, or Ann Coad as she also appears in records, was baptised at Lyme Regis on 27 February 1722. As one might guess from the letter, she would die a spinster, and was buried at Lyme on 16 June 1806.

Lyme also had its Dancing Academy, the social heart of the town, enclosing the gap beside what is now Alcove Cottage at the eastern end of Marine Parade. It is said to have attracted 'riotous behaviour' which was brought under control with the building of the nearby Assembly Rooms in imitation of those in Bath. Further west, catering for seamen from the Cobb, was the Marine Circulating Library. Its name survives as Library Cottage, with 1768-dated lead troughs and spouts bringing authenticity to what is otherwise mock-Regency style, as it was not rebuilt until the turn of the twentieth century. Lyme's first bathing machine, pushed out at this point, was provided by Hiscott's Lodging House in 1760.

Lyme's western landscape received its finishing touch when the Cobb was finally joined to the mainland by blocking the western 'shingle channel' between the High Wall and the foreshore, in 1756. Physically it was now complete, in its present shape, but Lyme was a dying port. By 1772 the decline in the lace and cloth trade, lost to the new manufacturers in the North, and a requirement for ships larger than those that can be built in Lyme, caused a great depression in the west of Dorset. A total of 118 homes around Lyme fell into decay and became hovels. Newspapers reported an absence of white bread, empty shelves in the shops, and the daily labouring wage having fallen to four pence.

The Revenue cutter *Sherborne*, commanded by Lieutenant John Cartwright (1740–1824) was operating from the Cobb in the 1770s in an extension of the sea war that raged against the vast quantities of spirits and luxury goods continuing to be smuggled into the West Country. Cartwright's experiences in Lyme informed his political crusade of later life. Having seen the voting system abused to the full he campaigned for Parliamentary reform. The town too was changing, despite the confident bustle of the third quarter of the eighteenth century, on the cusp of transition from former port to future spa.

Ships were already getting larger and the trend would be magnified tenfold by the coming of steamships over the next century. Even the big ports of the top league would lose out to upstart bigger ones, such as Bristol to Liverpool, and Plymouth to Southampton. Lyme's luck was to attract the social scene, to become third favourite to Bath and Weymouth as a watering-place for a combination of old money and the new rich, who launched their leisure lives on the profits of commerce.

The great libertarian benefactor of Harvard University, who endowed its famous library, Thomas Hollis (1720–74) of Urless Farm, Corscombe, also adopted Lyme Regis in the last few years of his life. He cleared a clutter of buildings at Middle Row to make an access through to the foot of Bell Cliff where he envisaged the creation of Marine Parade. Hollis was visited in Lyme by William Pitt, Earl of Chatham (1708–78), and his son – future Prime Minister William Pitt (1759–1806) – but local political power rested with the Fane family.

Lyme's two members of Parliament, returned in 1774, were Henry Fane (1703–77) and his son Henry Fane (1739–1802). Traders and Customs officials from Bristol, they were relatives of John Fane, 11th Earl of Westmorland (1784–1859) who belatedly restored honour to the family name as a soldier and diplomat, and as founder in 1823 of the Royal Academy of Music. The Fanes also appointed the town's Mayor and Customs officers. There was a whole raft of these including Controllers, Collectors, Riding Officers, Tide-waiters and 'Preventive Men', as Coastguards were known.

In all, 12 Fanes represented Lyme in Parliament. Lyme, however, was a royal borough, so the first call on a Lyme candidature rested with the Lord Lieutenant of Dorset as representative of the monarch. As a result a few others came and went at some of the 17 general elections in the Fane period, but always with a Fane, or a close relation, in the second seat.

Lyme was 'groaning under alien domination' as historian Cyril Wanklyn put it. In *Lyme Leaflets*, written in 1943 shortly before his sudden death, Wanklyn charts the downfall of long-standing Lyme names as relatives, retainers, and friends of the family were brought in by the Fanes. Town brewer Giles Davie (died 1788) was the last unchallenged independent voice as Mayor, doing too little too late to save the situation in 1776, after which 'old native and local names' such as Bowdidge, Burridge, Coade and Henley 'disappear and are replaced by those of men brought from afar.'

Even honourable exceptions had their problems. John Coade, appointed Mayor on 30 August 1799 and confirmed in post on 11 October that year, found himself side-stepped by the Fanes and the so-called Tiverton Act – a statute which allowed mayoral substitution – with William Peterson, Comptroller of the port of Lyme, effectively displacing him. Town grocer George Kerbey bucked the trend as an independent Mayor in 1780–81 but soon defected to the Fanes and allowed Customs official John Hamond to take his place. For borough council meetings and the Court Leets in October 'Fane cohorts trooped into the town'. As with Parliamentary representation the situation was self-perpetuating until after the Reform Act came into effect in December 1832.

The last great act of the free people of Lyme, encouraged by Thomas Hollis and his final act of munificence, came to fruition in 1775. It was just four years after John Wood had built the fashionable Assembly Rooms in Bath and they now had their counterpart at Lyme Regis. They were built at the hub of the town, after the demolition of old

Sea-facing stucco and thatch at Library Cottage, pinned down with older lead troughs and pipes, seen from the south-east in 1997.

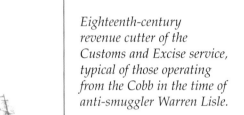

Eighteenth-century revenue cutter of the Customs and Excise service, typical of those operating from the Cobb in the time of anti-smuggler Warren Lisle.

Lyme's Baptist quarter included these cottages at Jericho, beside the River Lim, looking north-westwards in 1895.

warehouses at Cobb Gate, on the south side of the Square at the bottom end of Broad Street. They catered for the genteel socialisation of gaming and dancing, with cards and billiards being complemented by a ballroom. The Assembly Rooms, which were at their peak when Jane Austen danced here two decades later, survived until 1929 when the ground was cleared for a car park. One of the chandeliers was rescued for the dining-room of the Bay Hotel on Marine Parade.

Adjoining the Assembly Rooms, the town's Customs post at Cobb Gate was still manned by Excise officers until 1844. The gate was across the old Cart Road from the town to the Cobb harbour. Above it, the Walk has become Marine Parade, which is a split-level highway as a result of its double origins for commerce and pleasure. It terminates in a narrow street at the end to the north of the Cobb where Drayton's Bonding Yard and Store, rebuilt in about 1830, held goods to await payment of duty. Books and butterflies have since been sold from shops on the ground floor while the upper storeys have become holiday flats.

Lyme's local politics went through a violent phase in the 1780s. One meeting in the Guildhall had to be abandoned due to a riot, on 8 April 1782, and was adjourned to Raymond House in Broad Street.

Warren Lisle, the grand master of Customs and Excise, retired as Surveyor of Sloops in 1779 and returned to Lyme Regis in 1784. He proceeded to fall out with the town's powerful Fane family. At the age of 84 – as old as the century – he attempted to wrestle their traditional Parliamentary seat. They were his former associates. The consequent venom caused him to look back with sadness on his otherwise exemplary career as the most successful maritime commander in the service. Even his professional relationship ended on a strained note. He complained that his colleagues resented the fact that he had been 'too honest about the fraudulent practices in the various ports.'

The most successful maritime commander in the history of the Customs and Excise service, Lisle died in 1788 and lies in peaceful obscurity in the church of St Lawrence at Upwey, near Weymouth. There is no memorial to him, nor to his widow Ruth who died in 1790, other than a mention on the wall plaque to 'Anna Floyer, daughter of Warren Lisle Esq'. Lisle's lifetime seizures of £250,000 represent upwards of £50 million in present values.

The weather, as ever, was making news, although then if the climate was changing it was continuing to cool. On Friday 28 January 1791, a passenger on the top of the Western coach bound for Exeter died of

West Dorset smugglers as recorded by John Meade Falkner in Moonfleet *and dramatised by the BBC as 'Smugglers' Bay' in 1964 with Frazer Hines as John Trenchard (standing, left) and Patrick Troughton as Ratsey (centre, seated).*

Patriarchal resident and a visitor taking notes (far left) at Monkey's Rough in Jericho in the 1860s.

Monkey's Rough (centre) *and* **Higher Mill (behind, left)** *in a painting of Jericho by I. Mortimer, dated 1924 but showing how it had looked two decades earlier.*

exposure from the cold, between Chideock and Charmouth: 'He had been taken sick at Chideock, from the excessive cold of the foregoing night, but expired before reaching the next stop, and was removed at Charmouth.'

Dr George Mitford moved into the Great House at Nos. 45–48 Broad Street in 1796. The following year he won a great fortune through the National Lottery. He insisted upon obtaining a ticket numbered 2224 on the instructions of his precocious daughter, 10-year-old Mary Russell Mitford (1787–1865), who was adamant that the figures had to add up to her age. A short time later the counterpart was drawn and they found themselves better off by £20,000. Dr Mitford, an incorrigible gambler, proceeded to squander it. 'The detestable old humbug,' as William Harness called him, was eventually saved from penury by publication of *Triumph of Temper*, written by his daughter. Miss Mitford was among the best-known poets and playwrights in the land, although by this time she had moved to Three Mile Cross near Reading, living in a cottage beside a turnpike junction rather than in any style, as a result of having paid off her father's debts.

The Bethany Chapel carries on Lyme's Nonconformist traditions.

Bonfire Night on 5 November 1803 was an anticlimax at Lyme Regis after a fire earlier in the day destroyed 42 houses. It started at Crossman's Bakery in Monmouth Street and was immediately fanned by gale-force winds into an inferno that devastated the Coombe Street area and extended northwards to the Mill Green cloth factory, opposite the Angel Inn.

This area was the heart of West Dorset Nonconformity. Religious Dissenters traditionally used the Lim as their River Jordan, for baptism by total immersion, and gave Biblical names to their clusters of cottages and adjoining pastures between Coombe Street and Horn Bridge. Here, 'beyond the bounds of the borough and its bigoted burgesses', they founded their rural Jerusalem. Lyme's own Holy Land is still on the map with names like Jordan, Jericho and Paradise, although the rustic hovels have gone. In 1981, Peggy D. Yarosz of Stapehill Crescent, Wimborne, loaned *Dorset County Magazine* a painting of this area, signed by I. Mortimer in 1924, which John Fowles identified and described for us:

This water-colour is of the ancient Baptist cottages at

Jordan, just outside the old borough boundary of Lyme. The pointed roof in the distance is of Higher Mill, which still exists, though now flats. The fields across the River Lim facing the cottages are named Paradise, Little Paradise and Jericho, sure sign of a Baptist sanctuary in the days of persecution after the 1660 Restoration. The two cottages are un-tithed, a rarity in the parish, no doubt an added attraction to the original occupants, who would not have wanted to support the 'steeple-house'. The name Jordan strictly applies to the river, used as baptismal bath, but has over the centuries become attached to the general area in this part of Lyme. The road beside the cottages is the ancient via regia, *or King's Highway, and remained until about 1750 the principal access road to Lyme from inland.*

The date of the picture, 1924, suggests that it owes much more to romantic imagination than reality. The Philpot Museum holds older photographs of the area, and the cottages seem to have been in a dilapidated state well before 1914. This is confirmed by a rude local nickname of the time for the second cottage – Monkey's Rough. One early photograph, perhaps from the 1860s, shows a bearded patriarch, said to be one of the Hallett family, surveying the world from this cottage.

The Congregational Chapel in Coombe Street dates from 1755 and displays architectural confidence. The wooden letter-box in Norman House dates from its role as Lyme's first Post Office and was in use until 1853. The town's Wesleyan community held their first communal services at No. 34 Sherborne Lane, before the building of their Methodist Church in Church Street in 1839.

There are signs that the bulk of Lyme's unremembered lives were to be found in the former artisan quarter beside the River Lim, but many of their homes were destroyed in the Mill Green fire of 1803. Jordan Flats occupy the former New Factory of the early-nineteenth century, which was a water-powered cloth-mill. It took over from the Old Factory. Production went up-market in Victorian times with Silk Mill Cottages as the reminder that the 'throwing of silk thread' was the town's final contribution to high-fashion after the lace trade had its day. Weaver's Cottage, as John Fowles points out, was probably the home of the town's last weaver as once there were too

Coade-made casting in the capital, facing the site of the firm's Lambeth works, opposite the Houses of Parliament.

Belmont House, Eleanor Coade's home in Lyme Regis, looking northwards up Cobb Road in 1997.

The coaster Glencoe *(centre, right) at the Cobb in the 1890s, having delivered coal and preparing to load Lyme-made cement.*

many to make such a name both confusing and meaningless. It stands opposite the northern end of the Lynch at Gosling Bridge. Nearby, on the hill, there is the ruin of a fulling-tower. Using fuller's earth, the raw cloth was cleaned and thickened in these structures, before being worked.

Industrial Lyme boasted a remarkably creative businesswoman who made her name in the capital where she became an architectural fashion icon of the age. Eleanor Coade (1731–1821), who made it in a man's world, came from a Dissenting family of Devon wool and clay merchants. Descended from Samuel Coade of Exeter, they moved to Lyme, where they became staunch supporters of the Baptist Chapel in Silver Street. George Coad (the names Coad and Coade were interchangeable) was Mayor in 1729–30. He had 14 children including Ann Coade (1722–1806), a spinster living in Silver Street, whose surviving correspondence I purchased at auction in 1979. The same year John Fowles discovered the will of Ann's younger brother Samuel who built Bellevue, in Pound Road, in 1791. Now known as Kersbrook Cottage it stands opposite the old Lyme Regis Hospital.

John was able to confirm for me that Eleanor Coade I was Ann's sister-in-law and Eleanor Coade II was her niece. It was the second Eleanor Coade who began manufacturing a remarkable form of artificial moulded stone. The process was invented either by George Coade (died 1769) or his widow's Dorset father. Unlike modern reconstituted stones, Coade stone was a kiln-fired ceramic, with originals being moulded in ball clay from Devon and the Isle of Purbeck, plus added ingredients that were a close-kept secret. These castings were made to a scale of 13 inches to the foot to allow for eight per cent shrinkage during the firing. Tiny fingerprints on the mouldings show that children were employed in the work.

Coade stone received a practical fillip from a legal requirement – to reduce fire risks in the capital – that London's timber porches and exterior building decorations had to be replaced in brick or stone. To the surprise of builders they found that Coade stone lasted indefinitely, unlike painted stucco and carved stone, which quickly succumbed to weathering and flaking. Mrs Coade claimed 'a property peculiar to itself of resisting the frost and consequently of retaining the sharpness in which it excels every kind of stone sculpture.' It is a lasting characteristic of Coade stone that despite another two centuries of weather and pollution is still looks as if it was made yesterday.

Production continued throughout the 70 years of neo-classical Georgian fashion. It remained in vogue and was adopted by all the leading architects of the age. Remaining pieces in situ have been documented on 650 surviving buildings in Britain and around the world. Garden urns and statuary were also magnificent, in both size and detail, such as a figure of the classical maiden Plenty which was 5 feet 11 inches tall (having missed the post-shrinkage target of 6 feet).

She was moulded with a bunch of grapes in her left hand and a cornucopia, overflowing with fruit, in the other arm. A pair of spice-laden camels, each 4 feet 5 inches long, were produced for the Worshipful Company of Grocers in The Poultry, between 1798 and 1802. Numerous coats of arms were commissioned by companies and guilds in the City of London. One, at least, survives, but most of these generally unappreciated emblems were destroyed either in the Blitz or the even more devastating rebuilding that followed.

Sculptors worked at Pedlar's Acre, Lambeth, where the Coade family employed the best professionals in the land. They included the elder Bacon, De Vaere, Rossi, Flaxman, Bubb and Banks. Their talents ensured that modelling techniques and standards stayed first-rate and that the product did not loose its finesse. Larger items were given the firm's imprint 'COADE LAMBETH'. Mrs Coade went into partnership in 1799 with her cousin John Sealy (1749–1813). William Croggan, another relation, became works manager after Sealy's death. Production continued into the 1820s.

Eleanor Coade's will shows strong feminist leanings. She insisted that the bequests she made to females were to be given and signed for by the women concerned. This flouted the current convention which enabled husbands to receive – and keep – money on behalf of their spouses. Mrs Coade also showed favouritism to the girls in her life (giving them £100 each) rather than the boys (only £50).

The commercial success enabled Mrs Coade to return in style to her home town of Lyme Regis where she embellished the frontage of Belmont House, at the junction of Pound Street with Cobb Road, with friezes and panels of Coade stone in about 1785. According to local historian Henry Chessell, the house had been built by Simon Butler in 1774, with folly-like flourishes which led to it being called Butler's Castle. Cobb Road, built at the same time, was initially called New Road and then Coade Road a decade later. It became the access road to Lyme Cement Works, set into Ware Cliffs, between Monmouth Beach and Devonshire Head. Here the Coade chemistry turned to the commercial magic of hydraulic cement. Capable of hardening under water, this was the specialist product for rebuilding the Cobb and creating immense harbour works in the next century, of which the greatest in area and size is the Harbour of Refuge, which we know as Portland Harbour.

The notable Coade memorial in the capital is a 10-foot lion on the Lambeth side of Westminster Bridge. He was formerly one of the mascots of the Lion Brewery which was demolished for the building of the Royal Festival Hall in 1950. This, or a similar beast, guarded the entrance to Waterloo Station until 1966. Its present position is opposite the site of Mrs Coade's manufactory, at Pedlar's Acre, on the site of St Thomas's Hospital. Stone production has been revived in Somerset by Philip Tomlinson.

Wings (centre)
on Marine Parade,
seen in 1925,
was wrongly credited
as the house where
Jane Austen stayed.

Negative evidence of any link
between Wings and Jane Austen,
as it and the promenade towards
the Cobb (left) are absent in this
Daniel Dunster painting of the
inshore view westwards from
Cobb Gate Jetty in 1832.

Lyme's earliest photograph,
on an elegantly framed glass plate
from 1857, showing Marine Parade
in a view westwards from Cobb Gate
Jetty to Wings and the buildings
north of the Cobb.

Chapter 7

AUSTEN, ANNING, CRUIKSHANK & MARRYAT

Lyme celebrities Jane Austen and Mary Anning sharing their place in history with the Duke of Monmouth.

Having stayed at Lyme Regis in November 1803, when she witnessed a huge fire, Miss Jane Austen (1775–1817) returned to the town with her family in September 1804. Her tart view of Lyme society was developed for the novel *Persuasion*, published posthumously, in 1818.

Where Jane stayed still arouses controversy. Despite a plaque erected by town councillors, John Oldfield and John Fowles have shown that she could not possibly have lodged in the clapper-boarded house called Wings, on Marine Parade, as it was not built until after 1827. Wings was pulled down in 1945. Their 'logical preference' was Hiscott's Lodging House in Broad Street which was demolished and replaced by the new Three Cups Hotel in 1807. Further down, however, Pyne House on Cornhill turned into a more compelling contender

with the discovery that it was here that the Austen family broke a pot in 1804, for replacing which the landowner's agent, Richard Anning father of baby future fossilist Mary – 'made the exorbitant charge of five shillings'. Both Hiscott's Lodging House and Pyne House stood on the lower south side of Broad Street.

The evidence for having stayed here is provided by the novelist herself, writing from Lyme during 1804, as she describes the route of a walk from the Assembly Rooms to her lodgings. Having gone up the Bell Cliff steps she proceeds along the unlit Middle Row alley, above the Shambles, to this part of Broad Street. This short walk eliminates the other contender, the old Three Cups, as it stood immediately opposite the Assembly Rooms at the bottom end of Broad Street. Jane writes:

Jane Austen's bust and a misleading plaque on the site of Wings in 1960.

Granny's Teeth, where Louisa Musgrove fell in Jane Austen's Persuasion.

Marine Parade formed the Georgian link between ancient Lyme and its medieval Cobb harbour, with Wings being the white house in the middle, seen in 1900.

The ball last night was pleasant but not full for Thursday. My father stayed constantly till half past nine (we left a little after eight) and then walked home with James and the lanthorn. I believe the lanthorn was not lit, as the Moon was up, but this lanthorn may sometimes be of great convenience to him.

No. 29 Marine Parade, at the town end of the row of houses to the north of the Cobb, was known as Bay Cottage and is said to have provided the original home for Captain Harville who appears in *Persuasion*. The connection is perpetuated now as Jane's Café. An exposed rough-hewn flight of steps leading to the upper wall of the Cobb, known as Granny's Teeth, provided the visual inspiration for the dramatic scene in which Louisa Musgrove fell. Nearby, a recess known as the Gin Shop also takes its name from this time, but not for the drinking of 'Mother's Ruin'. The gin in this case was a hoist for lifting shells and powder from a magazine in the alcove to the gun battery on the harbour wall.

While Lyme danced, it was one of those new centuries when Europe mobilised to the sound of distant drums followed by the thud of war, giving rise to Napoleon who is quoted in military textbooks down to the present day: 'Always march towards the sound of the guns.'

Military affairs remained an intense local concern throughout the French Wars, although the great Naval victory off Cape Trafalgar on 21 October 1805 brought some relief from direct fear of Napoleonic invasion. In May 1806 the Admiralty Shutter Telegraph System between London and Portsmouth was extended westwards to Plymouth. The Plymouth Line, as it was known, was built by George Roebuck to Lord George Murray's design. All the construction work took place in the winter months, following the Battle of Trafalgar, despite all the difficulties of weather and terrain. Lookouts with telescopes watched the next stations in the line and, on a clear day, the warning of invasion or instructions to the fleet could be passed by shutter signals between the Admiralty and Plymouth in less than an hour. There were nine stations that spanned the centre of Dorset, being from east to west at Pistle Down, Chalbury, Blandford Racecourse, Bell Hill (Belchalwell), Nettlecombe Tout, High Stoy, Toller Down, Lambert's Castle, and Dalwood Common (since transferred to Devon). Several of these locations are still known as Telegraph Hill.

As in so many centuries, war and the weather were the main topics of conversation, with the climate on 15 January 1814 edging towards a cycle that presaged an Ice Age. Conditions were worse than anyone could remember for 40 years. The roads were many feet deep with snow and the mails from London required a chaise and four horses, arriving in Exeter from Dorchester – on the inland turnpike above Lyme – some 18 hours after the usual time. In Devon, a soldier was found dead at Haldon with £21 in his pocket; nearby were three members of the Renfrew Militia, also dead, and their bodies were conveyed to Chudleigh. From elsewhere in the country came news of deaths from exposure to the extreme cold. Seven boys were drowned on the Trent, by the breaking of the ice on which they had imprudently ventured before it was sufficiently strong.

Granny's Teeth and the inner wall of the Cobb, looking westwards in 1926.

The Cobb buildings and outer breakwater, in a primitive water-colour of 1820, looking north-eastwards to Golden Cap.

Below: *The Admiralty Telegraph Station on Lambert's Castle Hill, using shutters to semaphore signals between London and the Plymouth fleet, was a conspicious reminder, from 1806, that these were troubled times.*

Below: *Lyme nudes of 1819 in a George Cruikshank caricature of bathing-machine fashions and passions in a view south-westwards from a peeping Tom with telescope* (right), *across Cobb Gate Beach, to the Cobb* (left).

Cold weather even features in news of the discovery of a Roman tessellated mosaic, uncovered near Halstock in 1818, as it was accompanied by a note to the effect that frozen fingers prevented the antiquary on the spot from illustrating the villa floor. John Bellamy wrote in the *Gentleman's Magazine*:

I visited this pavement yesterday, about four miles from my house, having set out with the full intention to have taken a drawing for you immediately, when an event prevented me that I should most certainly have anticipated; the frost setting in severely deprived me of the natural animation necessary to complete my purpose.

In Lyme, the first of the thatched cottages to be built on Marine Parade was number seven, in about 1818. Madeira Cottage attracted a number of talented people including the artist George Cruikshank (1792–1878) who published an engraving to commemorate the visit. Published in London on 8 September 1819, it shows the bathing machines on the beach beside the Cobb harbour at Lyme Regis, with the ladies,

as was the custom, taking to the water without a costume between them. The caption 'Hydromania! or a Touch of the Sub-Lyme and Beautiful' was satirical, being a comment both upon the unfathomable fashion for cold water and Edmund Burke's essay 'On the Sublime and Beautiful' which was published in 1756. The steps down to the eastern end of the beach were known as Bathing Machine Steps. The nearby groyne, below Bay Hotel, was built by geologist Henry de la Beche in 1820, and takes its name – Lucy's Jetty – from the tidal Lucy's Ledge.

Naval captain and novelist Frederick Marryat (1792–1848) stayed at Madeira Cottage. He originally came to Lyme, all expenses paid, while working on

Above: *Heavy seas breaking beside the Buddle estuary in an early-nineteenth-century view eastwards to Golden Cap* (centre) *and Thorncombe Beacon.*

the adaptation of Sir Home Popham's signalling system, as a result of which he was elected a fellow of the Royal Society in 1819 and awarded the French Legion of Honour 'for services rendered to science and navigation'. He was also renowned for his heroism, having jumped overboard more than a dozen times to save drowning sailors, and brought a vivid touch of reality to his popular writings. *Peter Simple* and *Mr Midshipman Easy* led to *A Diary in America* and *The Children of the New Forest*. As for Madeira Cottage, its literary associations resumed in the twentieth century, with visits by the poet and novelist Walter de la Mare (1873–1956).

Additional thatched cottages had been built by 1830 and named Madeira Cottages. Argyle Cottage, to the west, was built in 1833 to provide indoor sea-water baths. On the other side of Madeira Cottages a twin-winged house adorned with hexagonal hanging slates dates from 1840 and projects towards what can often be a raging sea.

A combination of waves and weather enabled fossil hunter Mary Anning (1799–1847) to retrieve the

Madeira Cottage, once home to Captain Frederick Marryat, in a view eastwards along Marine Parade in 1997.

*Mary Anning with her geological hammer
and helper Fido.*

*The landslip to the west, between Beer Head and
Branscombe, which took place in the winter of 1789.*

Below: *The
undercliff at
Dowlands,
looking west-
wards towards
Axmouth after
Christmas
in 1839.*

bones of the great dinosaurs from the cliffs and beaches at Lyme Regis. Her father, carpenter Richard Anning (died 1810), started the trade and encouraged Mary to reconnoitre cliff-falls and landslips. Richard was said to have had an unfortunate habit of falling over the cliff, although he died of consumption, and Mary survived a childhood tragedy. That took place on 19 August 1800, when a riding display in the Rack Field was disrupted by a deluge at 4.45p.m. Spectators either fled from the field or sheltered under the trees. One of the elms was struck by lightning and three women and a baby fell to the ground. The women were killed. Mary Anning, the little girl, not only survived but is said to have been energised by the experience, 'shedding a dull demeanour and becoming highly intelligent.'

Ammonites were collected in quantity at Lyme and taken to Charmouth for sale to travellers on the through coaches from Dorchester to Exeter. *Cornu ammonis*, their current scientific name, became 'Cornemonius' in the local vernacular – amazingly learned given the general drift of the Dorset dialect – and 'Nartilus' was (and is) a *nautilus*. I still use it although the opportunities are unfortunately somewhat limited. Ichthyosaurus vertebrae also had their own name, probably influenced by the bramble scrub on the cliffs, as it was 'verterberries'. The ichthyosaurus was at that time beyond both the Dorset dialect and international science and ascribed to the crocodile family. *Dapedium* fish fossils, because of their shape, were 'turbot'. Primitive cuttlefish were (and are) 'scuttle'. What they called 'angel wings', however, were not fossils at all. They are multi-twinned crystals of iron sulphide.

Palaeontology was in its infancy. Animals preserved as stone were regarded as antediluvian creatures – the pre-Flood inhabitants of the Earth that had failed to make it onto Noah's Ark. Judging from the fins, paddles, side-armour, and sheer size of what is left (plus what must have been atrocious bad breath), it would be quite logical to argue that they are unlikely to have appealed to Mrs Noah. 'Fish-lizards' was about the best that early-nineteenth-century pre-Darwinian learning would make of the bigger fauna.

One ammonite never reached Richard Anning's shop as Mary is said to have sold it to a lady in the street for half a crown, as she was carrying it home, and then ran 'back down beach' to find another. Mary's personal acquaintance with the great dinosaurs started with the remains of what we call an ichthyosaurus which were washed out of the cliff by a storm in 1810. Having collected the pieces and brought them home, 11-year-old Mary sold them for £23 to the occupant of Colway Manor. Reassembled, as a wall-mounted display piece, they are now in the British Museum (Natural History) in South Kensington. In 1820, Mary Anning sold a splendidly preserved ichthyosaurus – as 'an antediluvian fish-lizard' – to the Duke of Buckingham for 120 guineas.

Lyme's Jurassic sea with a pterodactyl on a cycad tree, looking down on a plesiosaurus and a ichthyosaurus, with belemnites and an ammonite inshore and mare's tails growing on the foreshore.

Huge neck of a Lyme plesiosaurus, wall mounted in the Natural History Museum in South Kensington.

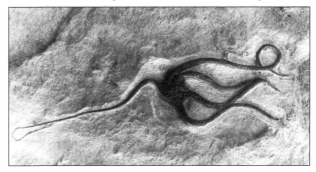

Lifelike squid in lias from Lyme.

Then in 1824 she found a perfect pterodactyl which was called a *Dinophodon*. That was a good year as it also produced a couple of plesiosaurs. *Plesiosaur macrocephalus*, the third, did not leave its greensand bed until December 1830.

Mary's father had exchanged views with visiting Swiss exile Jean Andre de Lac on fossils and geology. They discussed erosion which Richard Anning predicted would see the Parish Church slipping into

Ammonites, one in blue lias and the other crystalline, from Church Cliffs.

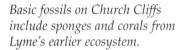

Basic fossils on Church Cliffs include sponges and corals from Lyme's earlier ecosystem.

Below: *Famous specimen, of a Lyme ichthyosaurus, wall-mounted in the Natural History Museum at South Kensington.*

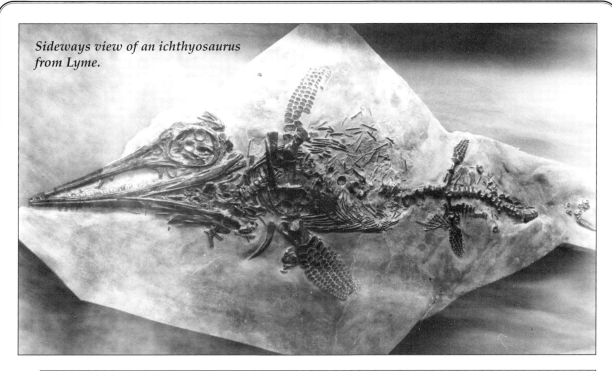

Sideways view of an ichthyosaurus from Lyme.

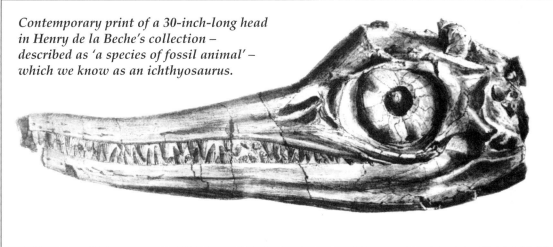

Contemporary print of a 30-inch-long head in Henry de la Beche's collection – described as 'a species of fossil animal' – which we know as an ichthyosaurus.

Active mud flow in fossil country, down the Spittles, in a view eastwards to Charmouth beach and a misty Golden Cap.

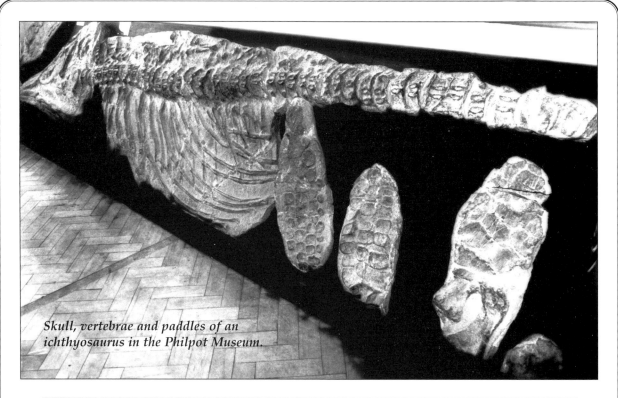

Skull, vertebrae and paddles of an ichthyosaurus in the Philpot Museum.

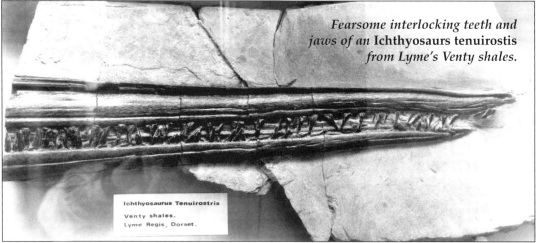

*Fearsome interlocking teeth and jaws of an **Ichthyosaurs tenuirostis** from Lyme's Venty shales.*

Ichthyosaurus Tenuirostris
Venty shales.
Lyme Regis, Dorset.

The Mariners' Hotel at the top end of Silver Street in 1997.

the waves – with the Anning family bones – if sea defences were not constructed. From observations around Lyme and Charmouth, de Lac believed the shape of the landscape had been caused by subsidence, but a study of the same cliffs by Sir Henry de la Beche (1796–1855) a generation later showed that the blue lias strata remained consistent with the contours on each side of the valley bottoms. He therefore proved that river action and weathering have sculpted the basics of landform geology.

Colonel Birch, a frequent Lyme visitor, had the most distinctive local ammonite species named after him. Mary had a working relationship with Professor William Buckland (1784–1856) who is said to have waded with her along the shore and returned with the fruits of an overnight storm to a late breakfast comprising 'beef-steaks and belemnites, tea and terebratula, and muffins and madrepores.' She is said to have held Buckland's views on anatomical science 'in great contempt' but wrote to him in December 1830 with her usual enthusiasm to tell him of a young plesiosaurus that, despite lacking its tail and a paddle, 'is without exception the most beautiful fossil I have ever seen' and 'every bone is in place'. Mary waxes lyrical, that if 'made of wax it could not be more beautiful'. She hoped to find the missing bits 'at the first rough sea'.

Mary and Buckland were friendly with 'the two Misses Philpot' who lived from about 1805 in the house that became the Mariners' Hotel at the top end of Silver Street. A century later, in 1920, Caroline Philpot gave Lyme its Philpot Museum. It had been built in 1901, designed by architect George Vialls, to ensure that the family's palaeontological collection stayed intact and in Lyme. Neither of the Miss Philpots, nor Mary Anning, were squeamish as all three brought back living sea life that displayed fossil-like attributes for dissection. The Philpot household had more space for practical science, and they were already maintaining the town's own reference collection, three generations before it became institutionalised as a museum.

Mary Anning's discovery of a flying reptile in December 1828 was the first-known British skeleton of a pterodactyl. The discovery of this pterosaur was published by William Buckland in the *Transactions of the Geological*

Society for 1829, although he notes that he had 'suspected the existence of the pterodactyl in the lias at Lyme' from remarks that there had been one 'in the collection of Mr Rowe' at Charmouth, 'about twenty years ago'. There were also fragments of a jaw 'set with very minute, flat lancet-shaped teeth, bearing the character of a lacertine animal' which he had examined 'in the cabinet of [the] Miss Philpots'.

Another notable pioneer geologist was Axminster's vicar, Revd William Daniel Conybeare (1787–1857), who witnessed the result of the amazing Dowlands landslip on Christmas morning in 1839 and became Dean of Llandaff in 1845. Lyme fossils were also studied by Sir Philip Egerton, the Earl of Enniskillen, and Louis Agassiz. All of them knew Mary Anning personally and were enthused and inspired by her discoveries. Those who accompanied her on fossil hunts were seldom disappointed but they had to pay for the privilege. Walking with Thomas Allan in June 1824 she found the dorsal-fin spines of *Hybodus*, or *Ichthyodorulites*, 'for which I was glad to have the opportunity of giving her half-a-guinea.' Lord Enniskillen revisited such memories in a letter to Sir Richard Owen in 1885: 'Neither of us, my dear old friend, are as young as we were, or near so active as we were when we used to clamber over the cliffs with Mary Anning.'

The Annings moved from Bridge Street to what became the Fossil Depot at the bottom of Broad Street in 1826. For a time at least, when the visitors had departed, real fish were said to have appeared on the slab beside fossil specimens. Impulse buyers were often outnumbered by a national coterie of learned specialists, such as the geologist Sir Charles Lyell, from before his knighthood. Mrs Charlotte Murchison acted as Mary Anning's agent from her London home in Bryanston Square. Mary wrote from Lyme on 25 February 1829:

I have got a very good head of an Ichthyo vulgaris *about two feet in length which I value at £5 and this day I have found a beautiful* Ammonites obtusus *about a foot across which I value at £1. Pray do you think it will do for Mr Lyell?*

She also supplied Lord Cole with outstanding material, but lamented the chaotic nature of his collection which he failed to present in viewing cabinets. In October 1833, Mary Anning lost her 'faithful old dog' Fido when 'the cliff fell upon him and killed

Above:
Lyme ichthyosaurus with the almost dolphin-like innocence of a species asleep for 65 million years.

Fossil-rich bands of blue lias Lyme stone, between beds of clay and shale, exposed in Church Cliffs.

Whitlands landslip, a mile east of the 'great chasm' at Dowlands, took place on 3 February 1840.

Thomas Seager's Fossil Depot on the south-east corner of Bridge Street, looking eastwards with buildings over the Buddle, seen in 1880s with the sign boasting that it was 'patronised by HRH Prince Alfred'.

him in a moment before my eyes, and close to my feet'. She adds that 'it was but a moment between me and the same fate.' The same letter to Mrs Murchison shows that far from being the confirmed spinster of Lyme legend she was looking forward to reading the presidential speech that Charlotte's husband made to the Geological Society:

I long to see it for Mr Hutton told me it was the best he ever heard and that Mr Murchison looked like a god when he made it, which I most cordially believe, for Mr Murchison is certainly the handsomest piece of flesh and blood I ever saw.

Fish fossil from the Jurassic sea.

Others noted the 'commanding presence' of Sir Roderick Murchison (1792–1871), knighted in 1846, who was awarded the prestigious Orders of St Anne and Stanislaus by the Tsar for his work on *The Geology of Russia and the Ural Mountains*.

Miss Mary Anning died of breast cancer on 9 March 1847 and is buried beside the north wall of St Michael's Parish Church, with her brother Joseph, who followed on 5 July 1849. He was 53 years old and Mary was 47. Inside she is commemorated by a stained-glass window and the inscription says it all:

This window is sacred to the Memory of Mary Anning of this Parish, who died in the month of March, 1847, and erected by the Vicar of Lyme and some members of the Geological Society of London, in commemoration of her usefulness in furthering the Science of Geology, as also of her benevolence of heart and integrity of life.

Mary Anning was remembered in Lyme as an inoffensive little lady. That was pure sexism. She was astute and assertive. 'I am well known through-out the whole of Europe,' she told the King of Saxony's physician, which was true to the extent that the Germans always took more interest in fossils than the English, as they do to this day. The interminable scientific arguments fascinated Miss Anning. 'I do so enjoy an opposition among the big wigs,' she said.

James Dollin continued to operate the Fossil Depot in Bridge Street through the second half of the nineteenth century. Jonas Wiscombe, followed by husband-and-wife team Isaac and Jane Hunter and then Thomas Seager, collected fossils on the Charmouth side of Black Ven. They boasted 'a beautiful stock' of ammonites and belemnites and 'eighty varieties of extinct fish'. Other Lyme collectors included at least one of the Miss Philpots, H. Marder, J.W. Marder, J. Harrison and Thomas Hawkins. The latter was said to 'carry away whole quarries'.

Hawkins visited Lyme in July 1832 and found that Mary Anning had just found the head of an ichthyosaurus which he called a 'Chirologostinus'. It became the largest almost complete British specimen and now lives in South Kensington:

Happening to arrive at Lyme the same day, I was fortunate in availing myself of the specimen. Accompanying Miss Anning the next morning on the beach, she pointed out to me the place whence it was brought. Persuaded that the other portion of the skeleton must be there, I advised its extraction, if it were possible, but Miss Anning had so little faith in my opinion, that she assured me I was at liberty to examine its propriety or otherwise myself. Hereupon I waited upon Mr Edwards, the owner of the land, and requested permission to throw down as much of the cliff as was necessary for such intention, which he very handsomely allowed me to do.

The sun rose bright on 26th July and the morning mists were hardly rolled from the hillside where many

Giant ammonite given an architectural niche.

Gravestone, on the north side of the Parish Church,
to brother and sister Joseph and Mary Anning.

men busily engage with spade and pickaxe to humble
the domed summit of this cliff. Progress was also made
on the following day, when people from the adjacent
country flocked to witness the execution of a purpose
which seemed to stagger their faith in our rationality.
By next day's noon 20,000 loads of earth, cast from the
crown of rock, constitute a good roadway to the beach
from that part of it which we had dug, and a few
minutes more suffice to demonstrate the wonderful
remain I tell of. Who can describe my transport at the
sight of the colossus!

My eyes the first which beheld it! Who shall ever see
them lit up with the same unmitigated enthusiasm
again? And I verily believe that the uncultivated
bosoms of the working men were seized with the same
contagious feeling, for they and the surrounding spec-
tators waved their hats to a hurrah, that made hill and
mossy dale echoing ring. Ah, but the tug-of-war! The
bones with the marl in which they lay, broke into small
fragments, so that I almost despaired of their reunion:
albeit with the kind assistance of Miss Anning, the
whole of them were packed, and by night-fall the last
heavy box was deposited in a place of safety. So secured,
the skeleton and its matrix weighed a ton.

In 1833, Hawkins returned to Lyme and bought the
rights to an offshore ichthyosaurus skeleton from
Charmouth 'fossilist' Jonas Wiscombe. After weeks

of waiting the prevailing south-westerlies veered to
the north and the cliffs blocked the wind. During the
respite the waves released their prey. 'Really the tide
seemed to gallop away,' Hawkins tells us:

Half a dozen of us – all lusty and eager for the
opportunity – meet. We arrange the mode of exhuma-
tion, dispose our instruments, and wait for the crisis
when the retreating waves shall desert the remain.

Once again they secured their objective. Thanks to a
warning from Mary Anning, that the marl will crack
as it dries, 'by the assistance of some clever carpen-
ters we secure it in a tight case with plaster of Paris so
that no power can now disturb it'.

Thomas Hawkins lived in novelist Henry Fielding's
old home at Sharpham Park, near Glastonbury, and
achieved the Latin specific name *Hawkinsii* on one of
his specimens as result of showing it to the eminent
anatomist Sir Richard Owen (1804–92). Hawkins, a
'worthy and eccentric man of genius', provided Sir
Richard with peacock eggs for his breakfast.

Sir Richard Owen became familiar with Lyme
fossils on sorting through the British Museum
collection, and he published *British Fossil Mammals and*
Birds in 1844. Lyme material also featured in the paper
on palaeontology which he prepared with Dr S.P.
Woodward for the *Encyclopaedia Britannica*, although

Use of Lyme stone, in Monmouth Street, with one of the most friable of building stones flaking away from its mortar.

Dinosaurland in Coombe Street offering 'Fossil Hunting Walks' in 1997.

the catalyst for Owen's work was a pearly *nautilus* sent to him by Dr George Bennett from Sydney in 1833. He also filled a gap in the fossil record by writing up the Mesozoic mammals from Durlston Head in the Isle of Purbeck, but rejected Charles Darwin's 'volitional hypothesis' explaining evolution.

During this time military communications were also evolving. The Plymouth Line of Admiralty Telegraph Stations, dating from 1806, were converted from their complex shuttered arrangements to the simpler semaphore system which was devised by Sir Home Riggs Popham and adopted by Parliament in 1814. Thomas Goddard began the survey for these changes in 1818 and Henry Maudsley of Lambeth was contracted to supply the equipment, with telescopes by Dolland, but the system did not come into operation until 1822. A new survey was announced on 15 April of that year which led to an entirely different line of semaphore stations to replace the existing locations.

The hurricane that devastated the Dorset coast at dawn on 23 November 1824 totally submerged the Cobb with an immense tidal wave. All the vessels in the harbour were either washed out or blown ashore. Offshore some vessels rode out the storm but the London coaster *Unity* was driven ashore on Canary Ledges off the Spittles and Black Ven. Captain C.C. Bennett of the Royal Navy, with William Porter,

struggled to its aid, risking their lives in the surging surf to drag ashore two of the crew of four. The Admiralty issued a statement:

Captain Bennett observed different vessels break from their moorings and drift rapidly towards the cliffs at Charmouth. He immediately provided himself with rope and lines out of his pleasure yacht and proceeded along the shore. When opposite a vessel that was stranded he got down on a projecting part of the cliff and was followed by others, particularly Thomas Porter [actually William Porter], a pilot, who, being secured by a rope, went on board the vessel and succeeded in rescuing the master, who was safely hauled on shore. Whilst this was doing one of the crew of the vessel fell from the rigging into the sea, entirely exhausted. Captain Bennett immediately slipped down the cliff with a rope round his body, and at the risk of his own life rushed into the sea and after some search succeeded in recovering the body, and with assistance dragging him safe on shore.

The rescuers were then joined by John Freeman and made repeated attempts to return to the *Unity* for the other two members of the crew – a seaman and a boy, who had to be cut from the rigging and dragged ashore. They were semi-conscious and battered and bruised from having to cling to the vessel for their lives. The *Unity* continued to roll in immense waves

Umbrella Cottage, an early-nineteenth-century cottage ornée beside Sidmouth Road, in 1935.

Detail of the oak carved door of Umbrella Cottage.

Ornate door and windows at Umbrella Cottage, looking southwards in 1998.

which were smashing over the ship and beginning to break it apart.

There was a sequel to the heroic rescue. Firstly, it was realised that the wrong Porter had received the credit, and that it was William Porter who went down on the rope to rescue Captain Pearce. Secondly, the three principal rescuers were awarded medals by the newly-formed Royal National Institution for the Preservation of Life from Shipwreck. Captain Bennett received its gold meal and William Porter and John Freeman were awarded the silver medal.

Landslip Cottage, looking northwards towards the crumbling cliff top in 1897.

Precariously sited, Landslip Cottage became an objective for the more intrepid Victorian and Edwardian visitors, along the coastal path south-west from Lyme.

The Landslip in 1903.

Path into Dorset, south-wards through the gate beside the Old Mill in 1988.

The Old Mill on the River Lim on the Devon border at Uplyme in 1902.

Rustic canopy for the wooden mill-wheel at the Old Mill in 1998.

Holme Lea Terrace in Cobb Road,
the home of Sir Richard Spencer,
who designed a self-buoyant lifeboat.

The Old Farm on Strawberry Hill, where Lyme émigré Sir Richard Spencer arrived in 1833
to found Albany in Western Australia.

Chapter 8

SPENCER, BERTIE, PALGRAVE & TENNYSON

The present shape and structure of the Cobb, re-clad in Portland stone, dates from its rebuilding after the storm of 1824. An inscription records that the work, under the superintendence of Captain William Fanshawe of the Royal Engineers, was accomplished the following year for less than had been budgeted. It cost £17,337 and ninepence h'penny. The length is 680 feet with the main arm being 12 feet broad at the base and 16 feet high. Fanshawe the Sapper retired with the rank of Lieutenant-Colonel.

The Government provided Lyme with a line-firing 24-lb mortar. This apparatus, devised by George William Manby (1765–1854), had already saved hundreds of lives and remained in use until 1878 when it was superseded by rope-carrying rockets.

Lyme had its own innovator of life-saving equipment. Captain Sir Richard Spencer (1779–1839) of the Royal Navy, who served under Nelson and retired to 6 Cobb Road, Lyme Regis, had been experimenting to improve the buoyancy of ships' lifeboats, by using several airtight cases made of thin sheet copper and encased in deal. These were put to the test at the Cobb on 15 October 1825. Six cases were fixed to a four-oared galley. Its plug was then removed as eight men stood on the gunwale. They jumped into the sea and then swam back to the craft when it continued to float. All scrambled into her in perfect safety.

Captain Spencer found life on land lacking in excitement and left England in 1833 on HMS *Buffalo* for Western Australia. There he became the first Government Resident in King George Sound and the founder of Albany settlement and harbour. His farmstead – the Old Farm on Strawberry Hill – is now preserved by the National Trust for Australia. In a letter home in 1836 he enthused over the country and its potential for food production:

There is no such climate in the world. Everything which grows in England comes to greater perfection here. I have Malta blood oranges growing here before my window on a tree which I brought from the island in 1817. I have eaten grapes, raspberries, currents and gooseberries from cuttings I brought from my garden at Lyme Regis.

The demise of Sir Richard Spencer epitomised the gulf between English traditions and Australian informality. 'Button your epaulettes!' he bellowed to two scruffy sailors as he summoned them to attention in Albany's main street. 'Button your mouth!' one of them replied. This threw Sir Richard into a near-fatal cardiac arrhythmia which kept him in bed for the next two years. He was finished off by a second massive stroke on 24 July 1839 and was buried on the hillside above his farm and the harbour.

Back in England, the new line of Admiralty Semaphore Stations was completed across Hampshire to Woodfield Green in September 1831. Naval surveyors had also visited Lyme Bay and decided on the cliffs between Charmouth and Bridport as the western end of its extension through Dorset. It was to cross Cranborne Chase at Rushmore and proceed via Badbury Rings, Bere Regis (Woodbury Hill), Puddletown Heath, Winterbourne Steepleton (Black Down) and Coombe (Chilcombe Hill), to Filcombe Hill (Golden Cap).

That, at 617 feet above sea level, is the highest cliff on the South Coast of England and forms the sandy-topped backdrop to Lyme's eastern views. As with so many things in the defence budget, however, these new semaphore stations were not proceeded with on grounds of prohibitive expense. By this time the first experiments were being carried out with the new Electric Telegraph system.

Lyme's place on the political stage began to recede into history with the passing of an Act to Amend the Representation of the People of England and Wales in 1832. From 1572 until the passing of this measure (better known as the Reform Act), the county of Dorset and its boroughs regularly returned 20 members to Parliament. Two knights were elected for the shire, and two members each for the boroughs of Bridport, Corfe Castle, Dorchester, Lyme Regis, Melcombe Regis (now part of Weymouth), Poole, Shaftesbury, Wareham and Weymouth. Between them these boroughs contained 1,225 qualified electors; that was an average of 62 electors to each member. This was now completely disproportionate given the under-representation of industrial towns and the so-called 'rotton boroughs' selected for relegation were those listed under 'Schedule A' of the Reform Act. Lyme Regis would no longer return two members to parliament as had been its right for more than 650 years.

Despite fading in importance, Lyme became a notch more accessible in 1832 when the turnpike road up Fern Hill and over Penn Cross to Lyme Hill was diverted northwards, and put into a short tunnel through Penn Hill. The current A35 takes the latter route, although the present dual carriageway now climbs through a deep cutting on the site of Penn Tunnel. Improvements to the road led to the introduction of more stage-coach services in the 1830s. By 1839, eight coaches a day were passing through Charmouth, and a pair of lighter horse-flies were based there at the appropriately named Coach and Horses. Changes of horses on the long-distance coach-and-four services were made at Winterbourne Abbas in the east and Honiton to the west. The next main stop east of Charmouth was the Bull Inn at Bridport. The route had its terminus at Pratt's Hotel in Exeter.

There was also a notable royal visit. On 31 July 1833, the 752-ton steam packet HMS *Messenger* towed the royal yacht *Emerald* from Weymouth to Lyme Regis in order to meet Princess Victoria, who was to be escorted over the hills by the Earl of Ilchester's Yeomanry from his family seat at Melbury House after spending two nights there. The 14-year-old princess was on a tour of the South Coast with her mother, the Duchess of Kent.

Thousands flocked into Lyme Regis from the surrounding countryside on 2 August 1833 to assemble on the Cobb in a dense mass, to watch Princess Victoria's carriage drive at a slow pace along the sands. Having dismounted on the western causeway the royal party was greeted by the Mayor, John Hussey, who advanced through a double file of Coastguards. The princess and her mother were conducted by the Mayor to the place of embarkation on the old Crab Head of the Cobb. A barge was moored at a floating stage to take them to the *Emerald*. The royal carriages were also put on board in the same way. Meanwhile, to complete the memorable hour, every available boat in the harbour was filling with onlookers at a shilling a head. It was at three o'clock in the afternoon that anchors lifted and the vessels were under weigh, with HMS *Messenger* towing *Emerald* with incredible swiftness. They turned westwards into Lyme Bay and headed for the Naval dockyard at Plymouth.

Lyme smuggler Jack Rattenbury, jailed at Dorchester in 1832, emerged to write his memoirs and become a romantic hero.

By now Lyme's traditional Nonconformity was being diluted by incomers and in 1837 the Catholic community built itself a church, just up the hill from the Vicarage, in Silver Street. It is dedicated to St Michael and St George. The Catholic resurgence caused or coincided with the taming of the town's traditional celebration of Guy Fawkes Night in which the effigy on a bonfire in the Square was of the Pope. Its lighting came as the finale to a virtual riot in which a mob armed with clubs and poles propelled and directed stacks of flaming tar barrels from the top ends of Silver Street and Pound Street into a sea of fire down Broad Street.

There was even nostalgia for what in 1837 was beginning to seem like a lost age. Jack Rattenbury, who was born in Beer, Devon, in 1778 and smuggled for four decades in and around Lyme Regis, published his *Memoirs of a Smuggler* which records the following courtroom dialogue:

Lawyer Bompass – 'You have kept school at home, and trained up your son?'

Rattenbury – 'I have always trained him up in a regular and honourable way, learnt him the Creed, the Lord's Prayer, and the Ten Commandments.'

Bompass – 'You don't find there, Thou shalt not smuggle?'

Rattenbury – 'No, but I find there, Thou shalt not bear false witness against thy neighbour.'

Bompass – 'Nobody smuggles now-a-day?'

Rattenbury – 'Don't they, though' [to laughter].

The sea remained the old enemy. In 1839, eight vessels were driven on to the Chesil Beach in a south-westerly gale, with the loss of all on board, but a ninth ship had a miraculous escape. The force of the waves at the height of the storm, threw this 500-ton vessel onto the very top of the beach. There she rested, high and dry, as the winds abated.

The George Inn at Lyme Regis, formerly the town's principal hostelry which had accommodation for a large number of packhorses, was consumed by a great fire on 11 May 1844. It was often visited by the curious, on account of the Duke of Monmouth setting up his headquarters there, after landing at Lyme on 11 June 1685. The blaze also destroyed the adjoining Customs House and old Three Cups, opposite the Assembly Rooms, in the Square.

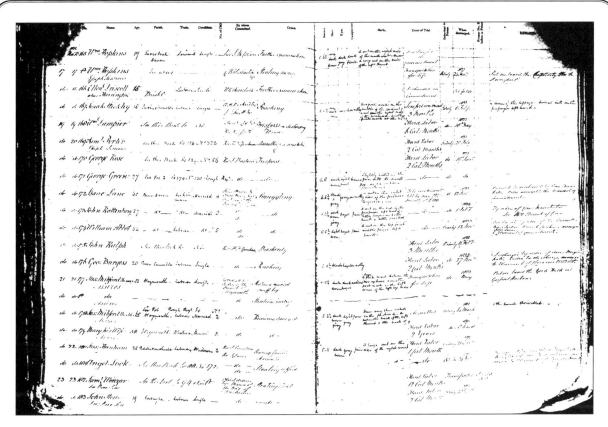

Evidence of Rattenbury's incarceration – as John Rattenbury from Beer, convicted of smuggling with Isaac Lane and William Abbots – with his entry as 57-year-old prisoner, No. 173, in the register at Dorchester Gaol.

The Square with the old Three Cups (left) and the old Customs House before both were destroyed by fire in 1844.

Market day in Broad Street in the 1830s, in a view down to the Shambles and its cupola which were burnt down in 1844.

A pre-royal Lion Hotel and Hawker's New Inn, Broad Street, photographed by James Moly in 1865.

Another casualty in this close clutter of old buildings was the Shambles, the town's abattoir, in Middle Row. This loss was generally welcomed as the cleansing of an obnoxious and outdated establishment. The replacement Customs House was also regarded as belated progress, moving to the bottom of Cobb Road, with the service having finally caught up with the westward move of the harbour in the fourteenth century.

The Lion Inn was another beneficiary of the fire, extending its frontage and declaring itself the Lion Hotel. Soon it became the Royal Lion Hotel as a result of a visit by 14-year-old Prince Bertie – the future King Edward VII – on his walking tour of the West Country in September 1856. The young gentleman, who was supposed to be *incognito*, travelled as Baron Renfrew, with Gibbs, his tutor, and Colonel Cavendish. They began their excursion on the Isle of Wight and he spent his first night on the mainland in Bournemouth, at the Bath Hotel, going on to Poole, Wimborne, Swanage, Wareham, Dorchester and Bridport. Lyme Regis was the penultimate stop. The trip had to be abandoned in Honiton after too many people recognised that the personable Baron Renfrew (one of his many lesser titles) was also His Majesty Albert Edward Saxe-Coburg-Gotha, the Prince of Wales. Newspapers reported that his behaviour had hardly helped the ruse:

The young Prince walked the streets with the jaunty independent air of an Englishman and chatted without the smallest restraint or with the slightest show of formal condescension with the poorest of the inhabitants. He had even entered into a personal negotiation with the owner of an extraordinarily sagacious dog with a view to the purchase of the animal.

July of 1847, in which year famous 'fossilist' Mary Anning died in March, was notable for the latest and last instance of full-scale election bribery in the far west of Dorset. Christmas came early to Lyme, having been engineered and primed by John Attwood, MP for Harwich and Lyme Regis, who was chairman of the Wexford, Waterford and Valencia Railway. The scheme led to lengthy hearings before a select committee of the House of Commons chaired by Lord Ashley. Proceedings stretched from 16 February to 6 March 1848. Evidence in person was given by a total of 82 people, mostly summoned to Westminster from Dorset by mail coach and the newly-built railway from Dorchester, and their cross-examination provides a unique insight into Lyme life. Tentacles of corruption crossed the Nonconformist divide.

Daniel Channon 'of the sect of the Baptists' appeared as the owner of a cigar shop and collector of Lyme's harbour dues. The shop was rented from William Pinney, the town's previous Liberal MP. Channon admitted 'a mission to Manchester' with a letter and asking George Upjohn, an unemployed Baptist, to vote for winning Liberal candidate Thomas Abdy. He had offered him 'a place in the Customs House, as a tide-waiter' but Upjohn felt this beyond his abilities; he asked for Channon to secure him work 'in the Post Office, as a letter-carrier'.

Despite pledging his own vote to Abdy, Channon changed sides on polling-day, and voted for a Conservative, Sir Fitzroy Kelly, 'within the last hour of the polling'. He had been canvassed by Robert Walker and Theophilus Burrow. Matthew Davenport Hill, counsel for the sitting member, claimed Kelly 'was the nominee of Mr John Attwood' who had acquired some 40 Lyme properties with voting rights – 'a very large proportion of the total number' – in order to obtain 'a corrupt influence in that borough'. Channon admitted that this was 'the talk of the town'.

The Mayor of Lyme, Robert Holmes, acted as returning officer in the Assembly Rooms on 30 July 1847. He confirmed that Abdy and his agent, Lyme solicitor Henry Franks Waring, had visited Charmouth by carriage to canvas that part of the Parliamentary borough (wearing blue colours). They were supported by Lieutenant-Colonel Sir Henry Bailey who lived in Lyme. Sir Fitzroy Kelly's agent was Lyme attorney George Hingeston and his principal canvassing was carried out by Dennis O'Kelly Templer (wearing pink and white). At the poll they were accompanied by brewer John Sellers and banker John Swaine Hook. The committee then established that although he was conducting the election – as 'has always been the practice in Lyme' – the Mayor was first to vote, and had done so for Sir Fitzroy Kelly.

Waring promised Mary Ann Farrant and husband John Farrant £10 towards the £11.10s. which they were struggling to find to cover nine months' rent. Mrs Farrant had gone out for a bottle of gin, to the Golden Hart Inn:

I had seen Mr Waring by the Hart, I returned back to my husband, and I told him what had happened; and he drank one glass of gin and water, and went up to his father's.

The significance of the Dutch courage and the paternal house call was that John's father, Samuel Farrant, was a voter for the borough of Lyme. Waring, obliquely but meaningfully, made it clear that they must 'say nothing to him upon electioneering matters'. John, a shoemaker, then found himself asked to supply the Waring family's new boots.

In securing his father's vote for Abdy, however, John Farrant had made himself homeless. On 27 September 1837 he received the following letter from builder Henry Jefford:

As agent to John Attwood, Esq, your landlord, I hereby give you notice to quit and deliver, on the 4th day of January next, or at the expiration of the current year of your tenancy therein, the peaceable and quiet possession

The Royal Lion Hotel, having capitalised on teenage Prince Bertie's walking tour in September 1856, looking south-eastwards in 1998.

Detail of the bay windows of the Royal Lion Hotel from across Broad Street, showing it finished off at the top by the plume-of-feathers emblem of the Prince of Wales.

of that messuage or dwelling-house, situated in the Butter Market Street of Lyme Regis, in the county of Dorset.

Mrs Farrant said that Jefford linked the letter with the bought vote: 'He said that it was all through me that my father-in-law went against them; it was after the election.' She responded that she did not care: 'The house was falling down about us; I said he was not landlord to live under.'

Abdy's campaign headquarters was at the Cups Hotel. The opposition was based on the opposite side of the street. Richard Sellers, a draper, described Sir Fitzroy Kelly's room in the Lion Inn, which he owned, and efforts there to secure the vote of book-keeper William Glyde from Bristol. It unraveled after Waring's intervention. 'Sellers, you have lost your bird,' he was told.

That was a rather neat pun, as, also featuring in the plot was civil engineer Henry Harrington Bird from Moreton-in-the-Marsh, where he was building a railway and had met professional canvasser James Birdseye in the White Hart Hotel. Here, coincidentally, Glyde finds a job accounting for 'plant, which is the wagons and those sort of things', even though 'he had no experience in railroads' and 'had never been on a railway'.

Bird's clerk, Samuel William Gibbs, told the committee that Glyde said he was 'bribed to vote for Mr Abdy'. Glyde also told him that he in turn had bribed other voters, one of whom, he recalled, was named Hodder. John Munday, a sub-contractor, then told the committee that Glyde had admitted taking money from both parties to travel from Bristol to Lyme to vote. 'He made a boast of it; it was his indiscretion.'

William Glyde admitted that both he and his father, Lyme voter William Glyde senr, had cast their votes for Abdy. 'Why was it you voted for Mr Abdy?' he was asked. 'Because my father wished me,' Glyde replied. 'Did your father, at the time of expressing his wish that you should vote for Mr Abdy, refer to the loan of £3,000 that had been withdrawn by Mr Attwood.' 'No, I do not know that he did.' 'Were you aware that there had been a loan at some previous time?' 'Oh, yes, I knew that there had been one.'

On making the bribery oath at the election, Glyde was heard to add, 'except what I had from Sir Fitzroy Kelly'. That summary brings us a third of the way into 366 large-format pages, which are packed with similar dialogue of revelation and denial. The charges of bribery against George Upjohn, Samuel Farrant and William Glyde junior were all found 'not proved'. Some general accusations of bribery were upheld but the result was allowed to stand although three voters were disenfranchised by removal from the electoral roll. The committee resolved, unanimously:

That Thomas Neville Abdy, Esquire, was duly elected a Burgess to serve in the present Parliament for the Borough of Lyme Regis.

That the names of John Wilson Cook, Joseph Dirk and Samuel Warren Puddicombe, were struck off the poll, it having been proved to the Committee, that they had received money upon loan for the purpose of influencing their votes.

The Committee desire to impress upon the House of Commons the necessity of putting an instant check to such transactions, which operate as a grievous snare to the voter, and totally destroy all freedom of election.

Culture vied with politics, in 1849, when the Hungarian piano virtuoso Franz von Liszt visited Britain and gave recitals at Weymouth and Lyme Regis. He was living with Prince Sayn-Wittgenstein in Weimar and composing his symphonies, before joining the Franciscan order in 1865.

Captain Willoughby RN, the district officer commanding West Dorset's Coastguards, wrote to the Royal National Institution for the Preservation of Life from Shipwreck in October 1851 to urge that a lifeboat should be provided at Lyme Regis. The case for Lyme was raised at committee meetings, during which it was pointed out that they thought the town already had one, in a reference to Sir Richard Spencer's experimental craft. Back in Lyme, Captain Horner's schooner, the *Mary Ann*, was wrecked on the beach immediately east of the Cobb harbour on 15 January 1852. In June that year the society asked Captain Willoughby what had happened to Spencer's prototype lifeboat. He replied that it had capsized, nearly drowning one of his men, as a result of which it was eventually dismantled and its copper air-drums sold as storage containers.

The Institution, having deliberated the matter for a full year, agreed in October 1852 to supply one of its Peake-type self-righting boats. The standard terms applied to the offer made this conditional on two-thirds of the cost being raised locally. Nature proceeded to underscore the need for the vessel before it arrived on station. Bound for Port Phillip Bay, Australia, in the colony that was named Victoria in honour of the Queen, the émigré ship *Heroine* came ashore in a hurricane on Boxing Day in 1852.

Her master seems to have heeded the advice in the *Pilot's Handbook* that when in dire straits in Lyme Bay they could head for the Cobb and 'run in and save life if not property'. Conditions were too rough for the *Heroine* to enter the harbour and she foundered on nearby rocks below Devonshire Head, between Seven Rock Point and Virtle Rock. The complement of 44 passengers and crew evacuated the barque in her long-boat and were led by the Revenue cruiser *Frances* towards the harbour entrance. The coastguard vessel was swamped, however, as they attempted to turn through the waves. Four out of the five of her crew were drowned including the mate of the *Honiton Packet* who had volunteered to join them. The hero who survived, William Bridle from the cutter *Primrose*, was awarded a silver medal for bravery.

The lifeboat provided by the Institution arrived at Lyme in September 1853. Eight-oared and 27 feet in length, she was housed in a shed below a sail loft on the site of what is now the Cobb Arms Hotel. The boat was manned by Coastguards from Cobb Terrace. Coxswain Boxhall took charge of the first rescue on 7 January 1854.

The Lyme Regis lifeboat was launched after a distress flag was sighted on a brigantine about five miles out in Lyme Bay. Eight Coastguards and four seamen crewed the rescue vessel as she rowed into a south-westerly gale. It was some considerable time before they could reach the *Jeune Rose*, of Bayonne. They found an exhausted crew who had all but lost their battle to control a vessel that was tossing from side to side with its hold almost full of water. The deck cargo was heavy barrels of rosin.

Seven lifeboat men boarded her and almost saved the situation, repairing rigging and setting new sails, as well as pumping out water. The brigantine attempted to tack towards Lyme. Then a particularly heavy squall rolled her on her beam-ends, as barrels broke loose, and the mainsail and boom entangled with the lifeboat on her lee side. This caused it to capsize, with two of the five men on board jumping clear, and Coxswain Boxhall and two others trapped underneath. They were unable to struggle clear for more than 20 minutes – when the brigantine partially righted herself – and then cut away the sails and rigging to enable the lifeboat to be righted. It then took on board both crews (with the exception of coastguard John Martin, who drowned when he leapt from the lifeboat) and sailed back to Lyme.

In August 1856 three men were in a boat that capsized off Lyme Regis. William Calloway, who was alone in his own boat at the time, came to their rescue and jumped in the water. He was able to save two of the men but the third was swept away by the strong currents and drowned.

The second emergency launching of the lifeboat took place on 7 October 1857. Twelve men packed aboard to give assistance to five vessels anchored offshore as a sudden gale threatened to sweep them from their moorings.

Lodging-house proprietor Thomas Bradley had succeeded Coxswain Boxhall, and Joshua Heath then stood in for a year, after which Bradley resumed responsibility and stayed in post until 1885.

The earliest dated photograph of Lyme Regis to be brought to my attention looks towards the new lifeboat station in October 1857 and is a view south-westwards along Marine Parade to the Cobb *(see p60)*. It is a silvery black positive glass plate, 6 inches by 4 four inches, in a small but ornate gilt frame which is said to have hung in the same house in Ozone Terrace, Chris Copson of auctioneers Henry Duke at Weymouth told me, 'from the time it was taken until the end of the next century.'

Dorset County Museum was keen to credit it to the landscape photographer John Pouncy of Dorchester, who was particularly active that year, but it is more likely to be of a Lyme provenance, 'by Misses Barrett, photographic artists of Butter Market.' The location from which it was taken conjures up an image of the ladies carrying their studio camera and tripod across the Square to Cobb Gate Jetty for their first outdoor work.

The first Lyme lifeboat was replaced by a new 30-foot craft, made by Semmens of Penzance, in 1860. Her first rescue, on the tide at dawn on 19 August 1860, was in aid of a vessel alarmingly close to the Chesil Beach at Abbotsbury. The 15-mile voyage took four and half hours to reach the ship which turned out to be the Dorset brig *Ceres*. Having lost her fore-top mast and several sails, she was only holding her position on strained anchors, which had her tugging and rolling. Lifeboat men were able to board her and mend the spars. As the weather eased at noon they weighed one anchor and slipped the other. Though crippled, and having to battle against a strong sea, *Ceres* headed up the coast, making progress at the rate of about one mile an hour, and eventually managed to reach safety in Bridport Harbour at seven o'clock in the evening.

The next drama was much closer to home, on Lucy's Ledge off Marine Parade, when the coal-carrying smack *Elizabeth Ann* was washed onto the rocks in gale-force winds during the pitch-black evening of 14 November 1860. As the smack became incapacitated and inundated the lifeboat manoeuvred between the rocks with the forward oarsmen holding her in position, by leverage against the rocks, as their colleagues saved the distressed crewmen. All three were from Lyme.

Inland, communications were at last catching up with the industrial age, starting at 9 o'clock on the morning of 12 November 1857 when the first train steamed into Bridport, thereby opening the broad-gauge branch line from Maiden Newton, via Powerstock. The single-track railway ran for nine and a quarter miles. The operating licence for the line was awarded by its owners, the Bridport Railway Company, to the Great Western Railway. Road transport would soon lose out to rail.

The Coronet coach was the last regular service operating between Bridport and Exeter, in 1859, via Charmouth and Hunter's Lodge. The fare was 12 shillings inside or 8 shillings outside, sitting on top. Hewitt and Company withdrew the service as a result of the opening of the London and South Western Railway via Yeovil and Axminster, on 19 July 1860. Local horse-bus services continued, however, with the most reliable being provided by the Defiance which ran with two horses for much of the year and four for the busiest days in summer. They were watered at the Coach and Horses in Charmouth.

The service began on 3 September 1858, linking

Bridport Station with the Three Cups Hotel in Lyme Regis, and continued in business until 1 August 1922, by which time it was among the last horse-bus services in England. The omnibus left the Three Cups at ten o'clock in the morning and returned from Bridport at four o'clock in the afternoon. Richard Williams ran the service for many years and William Hounsell and relief man H.C. Newlyn achieved almost legendary status as drivers. By the end of the century, as a result of the apparent ease with which he coped with the hills and landslipped roads, Hounsell was being called 'the best coach-and-four driver in the West of England.' The penultimate partnership of Vic Warren and Jack Walsh also won acclaim.

Six seats were provided inside and the same number outside. Two sat up front to the left of the driver – the most sought-after seats – and the other four were behind. They faced backwards with the sole comfort and protection being a cushion and tarpaulin. The fare was the same wherever you sat, Silver Street cobbler Harry Chapple recalled:

Bridge Street and the Pilot Boat Hotel (left) *shortly before demolition of the Old Fossil Depot* (opposite) *in 1913.*

No tickets were issued, you just paid the driver. They were kept going by Gapper and Son, the coach-builders in South Street at Axminster [from 1796 until 1939]. The buses were always in and out of there. In the summer the tyres shrank and everything started shaking apart. Brake blocks and wheel-shoes had to be constantly adjusted and replaced. Then in the frost and snow the feet of the horses would need roughing before they could turn around and come back over the hills.

Lyme's general carrier was William Hodder of Mill Green. The Hodders were commercially active across the town with Frederick Hodder making pleasure boats at the Cobb, George Hodder at the Masons' Arms in Silver Street, and Robert Hodder running No.3 Holme Lea Terrace as a lodging-house. William's cart operated from the Golden Hart, John Blagdon Pitfield's public house in Church Street, leaving at 8.30a.m. on Monday, Wednesday and Saturday. Its destination was the Packhorse in Bridport. Passengers were also taken at sixpence per journey.

Several railway-building schemes were promoted, and the ceremonial cutting of the first sod of the Lyme Regis Railway took place in Higher Early Mead, after celebrations in the Royal Lion Hotel, on 29 September 1874. All the schemes failed, however, and the line had to await the next century. Economic times were also changing, with lacemaking having died out in Dorset and suffering hard times in the south-east Devon towns. It was now being made by machine in Tiverton.

Bridport, Lyme Regis, and the villages of West Dorset shuddered from an earthquake at 03.35 hours on the first Tuesday of October in 1863. The rumbling sound was accompanied by a violent shaking of beds, like the passing of a heavy wagon at a short distance, that lasted about two seconds. Some thought that thieves had broken in; others awoke dizzy. The main oscillation was from east to west with a secondary motion of a whirling nature, producing feelings of dazed terror. Strong doors jumped open from their catches.

The shock was most violent at Bridport Harbour, Burton Bradstock, Chideock, Charmouth and Lyme Regis. Here in the westward communities many thought that their houses were being taken by a landslip. The fright was considerable 'though a violent shock in the early hours of the morning comes upon a populace deeply removed from the cares of this world.' Even so, to read of a great noise being 'comparable to a horse rearing in the afternoon', hardly makes it sound like a disaster of earth-shattering magnitude. Inland the effects were less perceptible but along the Dorset coast most awoke in the middle of that night with a vivid impression of shock.

Miss Alice le Geyt, sojourning at Lyme Regis in August 1864, was rowing a companion in the lee of the Cobb when she heard cries from the shore and realised that two boys had slipped from the South Wall. Miss le Geyt turned her boat into the hostile waters on the other side, edging round to the outer breakwater, and used an oar to hold the craft amid the foaming breakers as she and her lady friend hauled the cold and terrified lads on board. As a result she became one of only a handful of female recipients of the silver medal of the Royal National Institution for the Preservation of Life from Shipwreck.

In December 1866, the timbers in the relatively new second lifeboat at Lyme Regis having been found to have started rotting, the vessel was condemned and replaced by a larger, 33-foot craft. *William Woodcock* was the gift of an anonymous lady in Manchester. It would not, however, fit into the original fish-cellar boat-house, so a purpose-built lifeboat house had to be provided, about 50 yards west of the Cobb.

On 8 January 1867 it was found to be impossible to launch the *William Woodcock* from the western beach at Lyme into a south-westerly gale, which threw a total of five vessels onto the beaches either side of the Cobb harbour. The losses were the *Ann and Emily, Lyn, Maria, Spec* and *Vulcan*. The commander of the coastguard, Lieutenant W.H. Elton, launched the station galley and crewed it with two of his men and three seamen who volunteered. In fearful conditions they checked each wreck for signs of life and found that three had been empty on moorings, but two men were on the *Vulcan* and one on the *Maria*. They were all saved.

Fact met fiction at Lyme Regis in August 1867, when the poet Alfred Tennyson (1809–92), staying at Bridport, walked across the hills to drop in unannounced on the anthologist Francis Turner Palgrave (1824–97). He found his friend, sometime assistant private secretary to the statesman William Ewart Gladstone when he was Colonial Secretary to Sir Robert Peel, agonising over a manuscript in a lodging-house. Tennyson wanted to see the most interesting place in Lyme. 'Don't talk to me of Monmouth,' he snapped at Palgrave. 'Show me the steps where Louisa Musgrove fell.'

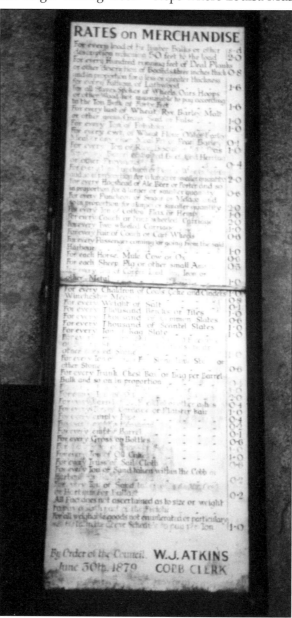

Landing charges, as imposed by Cobb Clerk W.J. Atkins in 1879, still in place more than a century later.

Tennyson took rooms at the Three Cups and was considering buying St Mary's, on Trinity Hill, between Lyme and Axminster. In the event he failed to clinch the deal, moving instead to the Isle of Wight, although Palgrave did settle in Lyme, buying Little Park in Haye Lane in 1872.

As well as attracting fellow literati Palgrave was already a famous figure, as the compiler of the phenomenally successful *Golden Treasury of the best Song and Lyrical Poems in the English Language*, which could be found in most households in the land. First published in 1861 it was constantly reprinted and eventually expanded in 1897. Religious quotations were given their own volumes as the *Treasury of Sacred Song* in 1889. While living at Lyme, Palgrave was appointed Professor of Poetry at Oxford, from 1885 to 1895. He was also a poet in his own right, producing *Visions of England* in 1881 and *Amenophis* in 1892, and he produced literary criticism, such as *Landscape in Poetry* in 1897. Palgrave married Miss Cecil Milnes Gaskell in 1862. She died in 1890 and he suffered poor health in his final years. They were survived by a son and four daughters. Francis Palgrave's brother Sir Reginald Palgrave, the Clerk of the House of Commons, retired to Swanage.

Western Lyme, looking across the Cobb harbour to the Palgrave family home at Highcliff (centre) *in 1997.*

BOROUGH OF LYME REGIS

A Schedule of Tolls Payable to the Corporation of Lyme Regis in respect of Goods and Merchandise for Sale.

For a Front Stall in the Butchers Market, per week ~ ~ ~ ~	1/6	For every person Hawking on Foot	1°
For a Back Stall in ditto, per week	1/3	For Pigs, each ~ ~ ~ ~ ~ ~	2°
For every Butcher Hawking Meat	1/0	For every Bull, Bullock, Cow or Heifer ~	3ᵇ
For each Stall at a Fair ~ ~ ~	1/6	For every Calf ~ ~ ~ ~ ~ ~	1ᵃ
For Two Stalls ditto kept by the same person	2/0	For every Sheep per Score and in proportion for less or more than a Score ~	5°
For a Nut Stall at ditto ~ ~ ~	6°	For every Horse, Mule or Ass ~ ~	6°
For Swings etc. at ditto, each ~	6°	For every Stall in the Fish Market ~	3°
For Goods Pitched ~ ~ ~ ~ ~	1/0	For every Boat with Fish ~ ~ ~	3°
For every Brush or Hardware Van ~	6°	For every Trawler with Fish under 20 tons	6°
For every person Hawking Goods by Cart, Waggon, Horse, Mule or Ass	2°	For every Trawler with Fish 20 tons and above ~ ~ ~ ~	1/-

By Order of the Council, Borough of Lyme Regis.

HENRY HENLEY
Mayor
20th. May 1872

Market charges in the time of Henry Henley, Mayor in 1872, with stalls at the fair averaging a shilling.

Impossible odds for Lyme's 1710-dated fire-engine (foreground, centre) on its last shout, to a devastating fire in Broad Street in 1889.

Natural disaster below Mill Green and the Angel Inn, a flash-flood having torn apart bridges and the Lynch path on Whit Sunday in 1890.

Chapter 9

GOULD, MOODY, WHISTLER I & LISTER

The extraordinary story in 1872 was that loss of life in an imminent shipwreck on a stormy night was averted at Stanton St Gabriel by what local people believed to have been a divine premonition. Isaac Hunter, a Charmouth fisherman, had a violent dream brought on 'by anxiety for his lobster pots'. He was in such a distressed state that he immediately dressed and set off to run eastwards along the coast for two miles, in the teeth of a gale. He found a French ship in distress, off Golden Cap, and was able to raise the coastguard and effect the successful rescue of the ship's crew. Their vessel became a total wreck.

Later in the year, on 26 November 1872, there was another heroic rescue when 14 men in a ship's boat, which was in imminent danger of capsizing in the offshore breakers, were rescued by the Lyme Regis lifeboat. They had abandoned their vessel, the Shields barque *Cassibelaunus*, when she foundered in the early hours off Start Point.

By mid-Victorian times, most of those we now call celebrities came to Lyme for its benign climate late in life, rather than having started off from there. One of the last great exceptions was the international ornithologist John Gould (1804–81), whose death occurred on 3 February 1881 at his home in Charlotte Street, Bedford Gardens, London. He was born in Lyme Regis on 14 September 1804 and has the distinction of having discovered and described more birds in Asia and Australia than anyone else on Earth. By finding so many new species – hundreds of them – he made himself the supreme birder of all time, leaving insufficient for anyone else to match his total until someone finds birds on another planet. Gould's hunting-ground spanned half the world, from the Himalayas to New Guinea and the 'Islands of Paradise'. The exercise was not without risk as three of his collectors lost their lives in the process.

His meticulous drawings, taken from the skins he procured or was sent, were to fill volumes. They were printed as hand-coloured lithographs with each being a work of art in its own right. These 2,999 illustrations are now worth a fortune, with the price of a set reaching £400,000 in 1987 and being so rare that I haven't seen a set since. Gould's other claim to fame is that he introduced the budgerigar to England. Lyme remains home to numerous members of the Gould family and about the same number of budgerigars.

In Lyme the symbolism of changed administrative arrangements followed physical reality on New Year's Day in 1882. The town finally lost its medieval port status. Henceforth, for Customs purposes, it was absorbed into the port of Exeter.

In 1884 the stables of Poulett House in Pound Street were converted into the Poulett House Chapel. The first minister was Revd Edward Peek and after his death the building became the Peek Memorial Chapel. Poulett House in Lyme took its name from an old Hinton St George, Somerset, family. After the dowager Lady Poulett in Georgian times, and then the departure of the Peeks, it became the Alexandra Hotel.

Edward Peek's other legacy to the town, given to St Michael's Parish Church in 1886, is a tapestry that was woven in Brussels in 1490. Peek rescued it, for £20, after it had been found walled-up behind a plaster partition in a house in Somerset. It depicts the marriage if Henry VII and Elizabeth of York. Churchwardens were worried about the care and conservation of their work of art so it was eventually loaned to the National Trust and found its way to Trerice, near Newquay, where I first saw it displayed in the tearoom. Revd Murray John Dell showed more taste and imagination than his predecessors and decided that Peek's treasure would do more good for Lyme and the nation if it were brought back home. He achieved this in 1996.

Lyme's royal tapestry, back in St Michael's Parish Church after being loaned to a National Trust property in Cornwall.

Landscape artist Percy Charles Porter (1859–97) of St Pancras married Bessie Boon of Lyme Regis in 1885 and moved to the town. He is buried in Lyme cemetery and two of his smaller works hang in the town's Philpot Museum. Lyme architect Arnold Mitchell (1865–1944) also painted for pleasure, although he preferred the greys and purples of wilderness areas such as Dartmoor to the local greens and blues.

The funeral took place on 2 April 1887 of colonial governor Major-General Richard Clement Moody (1813–87) who retired to Lyme Regis. He was the first governor of the Falkland Islands and later served in Canada where the Canadian Pacific Railroad named Port Moody in his honour. He also planned the building of the town of New Westminster. General Moody died whilst on holiday at the Bath Hotel, Bournemouth, and was buried in St Peter's churchyard, Hinton Road.

The Royal Field Artillery passed slowly up Broad Street in 1888, en route to Okehampton and the Dartmoor firing ranges. The gunners spent the night in the town. As many as possible slept on the floor in the old Drill Hall, which became the Marine Theatre, and the remainder dispersed to private houses throughout of the town. Residents were paid a shilling a head for providing bed and breakfast.

The town's historic fire-engine, provided by the Sun Insurance Company in 1710, last saw active service at a devastating fire which destroyed shops in Broad Street in 1889. It was hardly of any use, apart from damping down the embers, and was taken into retirement at the town's Philpot Museum.

On Whit Sunday in 1890 a cloudburst over the hills above Lyme Regis resulted in a flash-flood streaming down the River Lim. As it became funnelled into the lower part of the town it ripped out stone walls. The water level below the Lynch rose by 15 feet between three o'clock and dusk. Sheeting rain and hail accompanied the surge of flood water which fortunately coincided with low tide at the Buddle and enabled the river to thunder into the sea. Horn Bridge also survived the battering but wooden bridges were swept away and deep gullies torn in roadways. Repairs followed during Whit Monday in glorious sunshine. The rainfall of the previous 24 hours was recorded as 3.7 inches in Lyme, but it was estimated that twice as much must have fallen on the inland peaks from Hunter's Lodge Inn to Lambert's Castle Hill.

The Brixham fishing ketch *Rescue*, having lost spars and sails in a gale, was rescued on 7 November 1890 by the Lyme Regis lifeboat. Lifeboat men found her at anchor four miles out in Lyme Bay. They fitted her with their own spars and mainsail which enabled her to sail to the Cobb for repairs.

From exceptional rainfall and severe gales the weather then turned to one of the ultimate of old-fashioned winters. These were the norm in the 1890s and one was recalled as the 'Great Snow' for the remainder of living memory. The white-out began with intensely fine powdery snow. Carried by a gale, which reached force 10 during the night, it blanketed the West Country during the early hours of Tuesday 11 March 1891. By morning the blizzard had cut off the entire western peninsula with huge drifts.

The drifts between Lyme Regis and Honiton were 20 feet high and it was impossible to find the main road. The hurricane veered from north-east to south-east, and during the Tuesday the temperature varied from 29 to 31.5 degrees Fahrenheit, but it felt much colder in the strong winds. We hear that the storm centred on Dartmoor, stopping all trains below Okehampton and Plymouth, but the coasts of Devon and Cornwall also shared this indescribably wretched day. A correspondent from Lyme Regis wrote:

One of the heaviest snowstorms ever to visit the south of Dorset was experienced at Lyme on Tuesday. The town lies six miles from the nearest railway station, and the only communication is by two well-appointed three-horse 'busses'. On Tuesday the bus, with an extra horse, left the town at nine in the morning, carrying the mails. The conveyance, with great difficulty, reached the high hill known as Hunter's Lodge, where, notwithstanding all efforts, it was found to be impossible to proceed further. The one lady passenger walked to the hotel at Hunter's Lodge, while the driver, Mr Blake, rode back to Lyme Regis and obtained assistance.

By the time the luggage and mails had been transferred to a light wagonette the bus, except for the roof, was invisible, and the roof was only kept clear by the strong winds blowing at the time. Later on the same night, the driver of the mail cart from Illminster to Lyme started to do the journey on horseback, driving being out of the question. On about the same spot as the bus had been buried, the driver lost his horse, and accomplished the rest of the journey on foot, arriving at Lyme at one o'clock on Wednesday morning. Both horse and bus were eventually recovered and the mail carts resumed running on 17 March.

On the Sunday following the blizzard the body of a man named Bisgood, a labourer, was found near Offwell. He had not been seen alive after leaving the New Inn, Honiton Hill, on Tuesday evening.

Cold winters did not necessarily bring hot summers, but strong winds could be relied upon to rage at times for weeks on end.

In July 1891 a new 34-foot water-ballast self-righting lifeboat was issued to Lyme Regis. *Susan Ashley*, named for the donor's late mother, was one of several vessels financed by Charles Carr Ashley of Kingston-on-Thames.

The American artist James Abbott McNeill Whistler (1834–1903), who gained notoriety by suing John Ruskin for slander in 1878 and wore his derisory one-farthing damages as a watch-charm, spent a productive 11-week painting holiday in Lyme Regis. The irascible and pugnacious genius arrived in the

'Little Rose' Rendell was Whistler's
youngest Lyme discovery.

Whistler's 'Master Smith
of Lyme Regis.'

Master artist James Abbott
McNeill Whistler.

town in September 1895 with his wife Beatrice (Trixie), for the benefit of her health – she was suffering with terminal cancer – although she returned to Chelsea at the end of October.

Whistler I – there would be a Whistler II, also an artist, a century later – remained in Lyme to finish his portrait of the 'Master Smith of Lyme Regis', black-smith Samuel Govier (1855–1934), and his workplace 'The Little Forge, Lyme Regis' (now Woolworths). He completed nine pictures in all, including 'Little Rose of Lyme Regis', a portrait of Rose Rendell, the daughter of a former Mayor, who was shocked by his offer to paint her as she thought he meant it literally and would cover her body with paint. Another little girl to be painted by the master was Ada Case (1885–1973) who was immortalised as the 'Dorsetshire Daisy', and another child was entitled the 'Little Yellow Girl'. Both these paintings are lost.

The artist stayed at the Red Lion Hotel in Broad Street, although a few days were spent on the other side of the road, in the Three Cups Hotel. The litho-graph 'Sunday, Lyme Regis' shows the street scene looking uphill from outside there. The painter's studio was set up in the upstairs room behind 51 Broad Street which he shared with his companion Arthur Studd (1864–1919), a Leicestershire landscape and portrait artist. Writing to his wife, Whistler commented on the pensive and disturbed nature of his Lyme canvases:

This work may and doubtless will bear witness to the innermost of agonies we have gone through... how right you were in making us stay here – for if I had gone

without carrying these works on – I should have remained in the bitter fog – of indecision and want of pluck.

For, he would add, 'the one great truth that has impressed itself upon me is that time is an element in the making of pictures and haste their undoing.' He left Lyme on 25 November 1895.

At the time of Whistler's visit, the local brother-hood of the United Fraternity of Free and Accepted Masons of England were still meeting in the Red Lion Hotel, as they had done since they were founded. They were named Montagu Lodge (No. 665) for John Montagu Poultenay Montagu, in 1856. Their Masonic Hall was built in Broad Street in 1896. The project was financed by magistrate Thomas Embray Davenport Philpot, of Holme Cleve in Sidmouth Road. Tales from the Lodge include the story of an initiation ceremony that was dramatically inter-rupted when the Acting Senior Warden 'ruptured a blood vessel while the candidate stood before him'.

The Victorian and Edwardian list of Lodge Masters was later marred by the notorious deletion of one villain – unknown to us – whose shield was symboli-cally defiled and removed from the Lodge. It was taken for ignominious burial between the high and low tide-lines of the Buddle estuary 'so its remains never dry out, with the sea flowing in and out across them twice a day.' His 'disgraceful conduct' allegedly involved misappropriation of funds.

The best-known eminent Victorian to adopt Lyme was the surgeon Joseph Lister (1827–1912). His family had bought Highcliff House, on the north side of

James Abbott McNeill Whistler's painting of Samuel Govier in 'The Little Forge, Lyme Regis'.

Lyme blacksmith Samuel Govier at his forge in Broad Street in the 1880s.

Above: 'The Little Forge' – now Woolworths –
where Whistler found irresistible images.

Right: Shop fronts have replaced the Forge
in Broad Street.

'The Blacksmith'
in a Whistler lithograph.

Right:
'Sunday, Lyme
Regis' in
a Whistler
lithograph,
looking up
Broad Street,
pedestrianised
a century
before seven-
day trading.

97

Above: *Approaching the Cobb from the western end of Marine Parade in 1904.*

Cobb buildings in a morning mist.

Eastwards along the central section of a busy Marine Parade in 1906.

Sidmouth Road, as a holiday home in 1871. Influenced by the discoveries of Pasteur, Joseph Lister studied inflammation and the suppuration of wounds, using carbolic acid to prevent septic infection. He was created 1st Baron Lister of Lyme Regis in 1897, with the special lustre to the occasion being that it was bestowed in Queen Victoria's diamond jubilee year. The next monarch, King Edward VII, awarded him the Order of Merit in his coronation year, 1902.

Joseph's brother, Arthur Lister (1830–1908), was an authority on mosses, fungi and lichens, and the world authority on micro-organisms called myceto-zoa. His *Descriptive Catalogue* in the British Museum was illustrated by his daughter, Gulielma Lister (1880–1949), and she also drew the plates for Dallimore and Jackson's *Handbook of Coniferae.*

Arthur's grandson, also Arthur Lister (1905–75), married Sybil Palgrave and became the senior ophthalmic surgeon at the London Hospital. During the closing stages of the Second World War he served as ophthalmic adviser to 21st Army Group on the campaign from Normandy to the Baltic, and then flew to the Far East to hold the same position to Allied Land Forces in South East Asia.

The Victorian era was rounded off in style and with street parties and various good works for posterity. Tudbold's Almshouses, four cottages on the junction of Church Street and East Cliff dating from 1548 when they were endowed by John Tudbold, were rebuilt for the Queen's golden jubilee in 1887. To celebrate her diamond jubilee of 'the longest reign on record' the Jubilee Cottage Hospital was established in Church Street, in 1897, at a cost of just over £900 which included the building, eight beds, and a cot. After the First World War it moved to a bigger site in Pound Road. Lyme master mariner Captain Nicholas Marder died in 1897 and left £2,000 for the building of five almshouses for elderly seamen. These were constructed beside the Congregational Church in Coombe Street. 'A gift from the sea,' was how Captain

Tudbold's Almshouses, on the corner of Church Street with East Cliff, were rebuilt in 1887.

Marder beautifully phrased his act of generosity.

Inland, at Whitchurch Canonicorum, subsidence during the last winter of the century damaged the thirteenth-century Purbeck marble shrine to Saint Wite, whose Latinised name is Saint Candida. It is one of only two such martyr's tombs that have survived in the whole of England, so its displacement and subsequent opening and repair, in April 1900, attracted considerable interest. Inside, on its edge at the north side, was an oblong leaded reliquary, 29 inches long, inscribed '+ HIC . REQESCT . RELIQE. SCE . WITE.' (Here rest the relics of Saint Wite.)

It appeared to have been opened once before, probably in the sixteenth century, and had a thigh-bone placed at the top. This was 14 inches long. The other thigh-bone was missing, in accord with local tradition, and the bones were described as belonging to a small woman apparently of about 40 years of age. She was said by local people to have been killed in a Danish raid on Charmouth, but academics favour the alternative view that she was with Saint Boniface on a mission to Germany, when he and 50 of his cohorts were massacred at Dorkum near Utrecht on 5 June 755. The martyrdoms were recognised and ordered by Archbishop Cuthbert to be celebrated annually at Whitsuntide, which used to be the case with Saint Wite or Saint Candida, as she was alternatively known, at Whitchurch Canonicorum.

The sequel to this, at Lambeth Palace in 1912, was the discovery of a bone with a label: 'The thigh-bone of St Candida.' Its presence in London can be explained by the custom that when an archbishop translated a saint's bones he took one away with him. The shrine at Whitchurch Canonicorum, with three oval slits, still receives offerings of letters, cards and money, begging for her intercession on behalf of the sick.

The first motor cars to conquer the hills at Lyme Regis brought new heroes in 1900. Arrival was easy but leaving was entirely another matter because these vehicles had gravity-fed petrol pipes. Therefore they had to go uphill in reverse. On the steepest slopes they lacked the power to carry the driver as well. The only solution was to lock the throttle, jump out, and steer from the outside.

On 19 July 1901, when 13-year-old Bill Camplin went to ring the eight o'clock curfew bell in Lyme Regis Parish Church, he had the shock of his life. The body of a retired sexton at St Michael's, 87-year-old John Upjohn, was hanging between the bell ropes. Camplin recalled the suicide and his 'affrightened lad' notoriety for me from his Parkstone retirement in 1975:

My father made me go and touch the body so I wouldn't be frightened afterwards. Had he known how many dead I should see in the war he wouldn't have bothered.

Left: *Lyme's so-called 'volcanic eruption' in 1908.*

Cobb graffiti and newspaper cutting from the mid-1990s with Gabrielle O'Neill telling us of 'Fishy goings on in Lyme' as 'Film crews return for a touch of authentic scenery'.

Looking up from the lane at Cannington Farm to a figure 92 feet in the air.

Chapter 10

COAL, VOLCANO, RAILWAY & WAR

The new century brought exploration for coal and then oil, although the former proved much more elusive than the latter. What turned into a futile search was spurred by the realisation that the same bands of fossil seas rippled across the western side of the chalk massif all the way up through England from Lyme Bay to the North Sea. Over in the next county, towards Bath, the Somerset Coalfield was in its prime. So far, however, the mineral prospectors of Lyme and its environs had found no trace of black gold.

In 1901 a syndicate of speculators ignored geological advice and commissioned a team of engineers from South Wales to carry out the last and most determined attempt at discovering a Dorset coalfield. Their hopes were pinned on a section of shale cliffs on Timber Hill. They expected to find a coal seam at 600 feet but carried on boring to a depth of 1,300 feet before giving up. It was the deepest hole in Dorset until the onset of oil exploration in the 1930s.

Despite the disappointment, Lyme Regis was soon to be synonymous with fossil fuel, in the form of a burning cliff which was dubbed 'The Lyme Volcano' and appears to have come about naturally from the oxidisation of pyrite with the oil shale; a spontaneous combustion that can take place in these rocks. Pyrite contains 53 per cent sulphur. The cliff was burning, intermittently at least, from 1901 until 1908. Though it had continued to smoulder through the Edwardian decade, cynics claimed it was kept going only by surreptitious delivery of cart-loads of coal, courtesy of the town's hoteliers, who had no wish to see the life go out of a tourist attraction.

Public transport to Lyme Regis at the beginning of the twentieth century was much as it had been for centuries. The horse-bus service between Charmouth and Axminster continued until 1911, operated by Joe Taylor and son Archibald, and was then motorised with an improvised eight-seat open-air Daimler touring car. This, like its predecessor service, came no closer to Lyme than the foot of Charmouth Hill. The mainline railway from London arrived at Axminster in 1860 but no regular horse-bus link was provided to Lyme until John Groves of the Royal Lion Hotel took the initiative in the late 1870s.

He made an agency deal with the London and South Western Railway and the bus went to Axminster Station twice a day to meet the busiest trains (arriving at 12.57 and 15.08 hours). It was known as the Lyme Regis Railway Bus. Drivers included Harry Blake, Bill Blake, Tom Woodman, Harry Groves and Jim Steward. 'To all over the World and Other Foreign Parts' was chalked on its side panels.

The service continued until the late arrival on Dorset's western seaboard, in August 1903, of Lyme's own railway line. Failed schemes dated back to 1845. The main sponsors in 1899 of the line that was built were the banker Colonel Robert Williams of Bridehead at Littlebredy, Sir John Kennaway MP, H.H.J.W. Drummond, Frederic Julius Macaulay and H.G.S. Williams. They established the Axminster and Lyme Regis Light Railway Company. The local director was John Reginald Charles Talbot of Rhode Hill, Lyme Regis, and they won the support of the principal landowner, Sir Wilfrid Peek at Rousdon.

Technically, this was a light railway, although built to standard-gauge specifications. Sinuous, curving and climbing, it stretched 6 miles 59 chains, through the deep-cut valleys of south-east Devon. The biggest of these was bridged with a great concrete viaduct between Cannington and Combpyne which was 609 feet long, and 93 feet high, supported on nine piers. From 1-in-40 in the cutting after Combpyne Station, at 470 feet above sea level, the gradient eased to 1-in-94 and then stiffened to 1-in-80 over Combpyne Viaduct. Despite the scale of the engineering – and including land purchases – the line construction cost was a reasonable £67,000.

Arthur Pain was the engineer and contractors Baldry and Yerburgh of Westminster imported materials, via the Cobb at Lyme, on the ketch *Ida*. Work began in August 1900. Pain rigged an overhead cable-way to cross the valley at Cannington and decided that as Lyme had a cement works he would rely on concrete as 'the new material for a new century'. His inspiration, clearly visible to rail passengers between Christchurch and Brockenhurst, was the 218-foot Arnewood Tower, near Sway. Built in 1877 by Andrew Thomas Turton Peterson, a retired judge of the High Court of Calcutta, this demonstrated the value of cement as a building material. It had never been tested before on such a scale – 14 storeys with a spiral staircase of 330 steps – using only unskilled local labour. Judge Peterson prepared all his own engineering specifications, although

Combpyne Viaduct, above Cannington Farm,
survived the Beeching axe.

Arch details, with horizontal lines from the timber
shuttering which held the concrete.

Lyme Regis Station and engine No. 227 (left) in 1907.

without much difficulty as he claimed to be in receipt of 'spirit directions' from Sir Christopher Wren, who died in 1723. The Cannington viaduct became its linear equivalent.

Pain also offered to encase Lyme's historic Cobb in concrete and revive Victorian aspirations to 'increase the acreage of water in Lyme Regis harbour', but the Edwardian picture postcard was spreading its charms and the project failed to materialise. The single-track Axminster and Lyme Regis Light Railway had a passing loop at Combpyne Station and its junction, with the London and South Western Railway, beside the up-platform at Axminster Station (having crossed the mainline by an iron bridge). This was 144 miles 66 chains from Waterloo. There was also an eastern loop from the Lyme side of the bridge, beside the goods yard, which joined the down-line. This was lifted in 1915.

Arthur Pain's 'work-horse' – his construction engine – was 0-6-0ST saddle-tank Number 135 of the old 330-class, but she was unsuitable for working passenger trains throughout the day. Operational locomotives were provided by the London and South Western Railway and had their depot at Exmouth Junction. These initially were two 0-6-0 Brighton-built 0-6-0T Terrier tank engines, built in 1874 and 1876 to a design by William Stroudley for the London, Brighton and South Coast Railway. A pair were needed to double-head trains of more than three coaches.

The 1874-built engine (originally numbered 68 and named *Clapham*) was given the number 735 on being bought for the Lyme line. Her 1876-built partner (original Number 46, named *Newington*) was re-numbered 734. Both were soon moved on, after it was noticed that the sharp curves caused wheel damage, with *Newington* becoming British Railways engine 32646 *Freshwater*, on the Isle of Wight. In retirement she is the static *Hayling Billy*, on Hayling Island in Hampshire.

The line was sold to the London and South Western Railway on 31 December 1906. Designed by William Adams, O2-class 0-4-2T tank engines were the next to work it, until the middle of the First World War. Numbers 227 and 230 regularly serviced the line. Their successors, Adams 4-2-2T Jubilee-class Glasgow-built radial tank engines, dated from 1885 and carried the numbers 125 and 520. They continued to work the line into the second half of the century but were frequently re-numbered as shown below, which is of more than academic interest as such numbers are often the only way of identifying otherwise featureless photographs.

$$125 = 0125 = 3125 = 30582$$
$$520 = 0520 = 3520 = 30584$$

Four ex-Brighton Stroudley D1 0-4-2T tank engines joined them in the winter of 1928. Their numbers were 276, 359, 612 and 633. These soon succumbed the wheel wear on the tight curves and were withdrawn in the 1930s. The lasting postwar addition, arriving in 1946 from the East Kent Railway, was Adams 4-4-2T tank locomotive Number 5, given LSWR Number 488. Glasgow-built by Neilson in 1885, she had the same specification and dimensions as 125 and 520. She also went through the following number changes in subsequent nationalisation and eventual preservation, being sold to the Bluebell Railway at Brighton, in 1961:

$$5 = 488 = 3488 = 30583 = 488$$

Other locomotives visited the line, such as O2-class 0-4-4 engines, but could only operate with partially-filled tanks in order to comply with weight restrictions. M7-class 0-4-4T engines, designed by H.G. Ivatt, appeared on the line during the dying days of steam. No. 41291 was a regular visitor. The locomotive that never arrived was mainline 4-6-2 Pacific-type Number 21C109 which was named *Lyme Regis* in honour of the town as one of the West Country Class. Because of her weight and size, the closest she could come to the town was Axminster, for Alderman H.I. Blanchard to unveil her name-plate in August 1946.

The original timetable for weekdays, starting on Monday 24 August 1903, was for six trains a day in each direction between Lyme Regis and Axminster, with intermediate stops at Combpyne. As with the buses there was no Sunday service (until 30 June 1930). Travelling time from Lyme Regis to Axminster was 25 minutes. Maximum speed was 25 miles per hour, reduced to 15 mph over Cannington viaduct, and 10 mph on the acute curves. The whole journey, onwards to Waterloo, took 4 hours 10 minutes. The maximum permitted load per locomotive was 120 tons. Five coaches fitted in the platform bay on the north side of the up-line at Axminster. Occasionally the mainline hosted three coaches from Lyme Regis to Waterloo – attached to through trains at Axminster – on the busiest summer Saturdays. This was the traditional 'change-over day' for holiday-makers in hotels and guest-houses. A real rarity was an intact train that arrived in Lyme from distant parts, such as that bringing Oldham Boys' Brigade for their annual summer camp, which then waited in a goods siding till they were ready to return 'up North'.

The station plate at Lyme Regis read 'Lyme Regis (for Charmouth)' and that at the midway stop carried the name-plate 'Combpyne (for the Landslip)'. Opening-day celebrations concentrated on garlanded locomotive No. 735 piloting No. 734 as she worked the 12.25 up-train from Lyme Regis. It left to chiming church bells and the Artillery Band playing beside the tracks. Having lingered for the breathtaking view from the ten-arch Cannington viaduct, Lyme's dignitaries were met in Axminster by Sir John Kennaway and massed ranks of the Parish Council and traders,

Lyme's newly opened Edwardian station.

to rousing renditions of 'See the Conquering Hero Comes', 'Rule Britannia' and 'God save the King' by the Pride of Axe Band. The chairman of Axminster Parish Council, solicitor W.H. Pitfield Chapple, provided the champagne.

Despite the wonders of concrete the Cannnington viaduct – 'built on quicksand,' Pitfield Chapple admitted – soon sagged and had to have its third arch from the western end propped by an inner double jack-arch. The line had come late in the railway age and coincided with motor vehicles conquering western hills. It therefore caused little surprise that Lyme Regis was among the 2,300 stations recommended for closure by Dr Richard Beeching in 1963. Operations were reduced to a push-and-pull shuttle with a single coach, and diesel multiple units then replaced the steam engines. The last steam visitors were ex-London Midland Scottish 2-6-2T locomotives Numbers 41217 and 41291. The latter brought the Locomotive Club of Great Britain for their nostalgic and tearful 'Goodbye' tour of East Devon lines on 28 February 1965. The branch from Axminster was doomed and its last trains ran on 29 November 1965. Its track was lifted in 1967 and an attempt at resurrecting the line, from Combpyne Station to Axminster on narrow-gauge rails, was a commercial failure.

Combpyne Station became a private house. Cannington viaduct still stands. Bradford's builders' merchants bought Lyme Regis Station and used de-wheeled goods wagons as storage sheds on the former loading bays. The main station buildings remained until 1979 and were then removed with archaeological

precision, each piece being photographed and numbered, for re-erection and an afterlife at Alresford Station on the preserved section of the Mid-Hants Railway between Winchester and Alton.

Lyme's little railway came too late to bring relief to the town in the severe winters of the 1880s and '90s but it lasted long enough for a triumphal swansong. The last great winter of the millennium began with a foot of snow after 26 December 1962. This was freeze-dried by the most prolonged sub-zero temperatures since 1740 and glistened in the moonlight as the snow lay on the ground for a record 70 days. Packed drifts remained several feet deep between the hedgerows of green lanes until Easter 1963. Lyme's lifeline kept running throughout, with a lone M7 engine going backwards and forwards as an improvised snow-plough, and the staff were heroic. One of the drivers and his fireman came across the fields from Axmouth every day, avoiding the drifts on blocked roads, and another member of staff came over the fields from Kilmington, on the other side of the River Axe. The snow made the ground visible throughout the cold nights although that was little comfort for those who set their alarm clocks for 3.30a.m.

The railway came and went with its traditions held high. No one would boast that it was a 'safe line' but it had been just that. Mishaps that occurred were always in the trivial category. There had been no death or serious accident involving either passengers or railwaymen.

As with the late arrival of the railway, so too with Langmoor Gardens, as the town's Edwardian park is

The single platform at Lyme Regis, looking south-westwards to the station, with cultural graffiti for Dame Janet Baker in 1976.

Lyme Regis Station before removal to its new home on a steam railway at Alresford.

Railway land in limbo, across the former goods yards at Lyme Regis, in 1976.

known, on the hillside above Marine Parade. They were provided in 1910 from a bequest by John Moly of Langmoor, near Charmouth.

The Edwardian age bowed out with hands across the sea to help the German barque *Furst Bismarck* from Bremen. That she was able to proceed, westwards down the Channel, was due to Lyme lifeboat Coxswain Bob Abbott – full name Robert West Abbott – who handled lifeboat *Susan Ashley* from 1903 and her successor until 1925. Despite having dropped anchors, these were dragging and the Germans found themselves driven on to a lee shore by strong south-easterly winds, as *Susan Ashley* rowed to her aid at 21.40 hours on 27 November 1910.

The Germans quite expected the barque to be beached and broken up. They asked Abbott to stand by through the night to take them off when the situation deteriorated. To their relief and surprise, the wind dropped overnight, and instead of being taken off they were joined at dawn by lifeboat men who struggled with the crew to weigh anchors. *Furst Bismarck* headed onwards and outwards, across the Atlantic, to the British Caribbean island of Trinidad. There was already a rising tide of diplomatic uncertainty in the year that 'Edward the Peacemaker', who visited Lyme as Prince Bertie, died and was succeeded by the 'Sailor King' George V. Ironically, recalling that uncomfortable night a few years later, Bob Abbott wondered how many of the German crew were now in U-boats and the enemy's High Seas Fleet.

The new motorised age was not only contained by the hills but constrained by a huddle of old buildings at the bottom of Broad Street, into which a variety of vehicles had collided.

The widening of the Buddle Bridge at Lyme in April 1912 uncovered an older Norman structure, of several stone arches, across a much wider Lim estuary. The later bridge dated from the fourteenth century. Work continued in 1913 with the demolition of a range of dilapidated cottages, including the Fossil Depot, revealing the wood tracery window and recessed aumbry of a priest's chamber on the south-west side of the original bridge. The room was sizeable, measuring 20 feet by 19 feet 6 inches, with steps leading down to traces of a lower cell or boathouse at water level. This has already been mentioned as a link with pre-Reformation salt dues and bridge tolls collected on behalf of the Abbot of Sherborne.

Fifty years of gathering tensions in Europe were leading to five days that changed history. Queen Victoria may have been 'sure that Germany would be the safest ally in every way', but Bismarck's foreign policy was centred in a triangle with Britain, France and Russia making up sides of varying size. What he gained from Britain during diplomatic entente, out of all proportion to its size, was the cession of the strategic Heligoland islands – off Cuxhaven at the mouth of the Elbe – which proved of inestimable value to the German Navy.

Europe imploded when the Austro-Hungarian empire fell apart in the Balkans. Six bombs, prepared

Donkey, beach tents and visitors during the summer which ended with the outbreak of war, 1914.

for the attack on Archduke Franz Ferdinand in Sarajevo, on 28 June 1914, came from the Royal Serbian Arsenal at Kragujevac. They 'had the appearance of pieces of soap'. Only one was thrown, missing the Archducal motor car, and the assassinations of Franz Ferdinand and Duchess Sophie of Hohenberg were carried out by student Gavrilo Princip with two shots from a Browning pistol.

Diplomatic steps to avoid the build-up to war fell apart on 31 July 1914. German ambassadors declared that if the Russian Government did not stop its general mobilisation within 12 hours, then Germany would also mobilise. The next question was whether the French would remain neutral. German mobilisation was on two fronts – east and west – and as France's ally, Britain also ceased to be 'neutral terrain'. War against Germany was announced in the House of Commons by Sir Edward Grey, the Secretary of State for Foreign Affairs, on 4 August 1914.

Lyme's direct experience of war was at sea. In the initial excitement, as the War Office commandeered the best horses in the county, medieval beacon points were re-established. First off the mark was the owner of the Manor House at Wootton Fitzpaine who became Captain Douglas Pass (1885–1970) of the 1st Dorset Yeomanry in 1915. The secretary of the Cattistock Hunt, his war began by marshalling his estate clerk, Samuel Hansford, and head gamekeeper, Thomas Havis, to muster their servants and villagers. A convoy of wagons, hauled by cart-horses, carried combustible materials to Thorncombe Beacon where a rota of volunteers kept vigil for the sight of other fires. Runners prepared to rush down the hill to ring the church bells in Chideock if German raiders were sighted. The next beacons along Lyme Bay were on East Cliff, above West Bay, and in the ancient earthworks of Abbotsbury Castle. Captain Pass later explained the thinking behind the plan:

At that time it was considered possible that a German raiding party might land on our coast and their first move would be to cut the telegraph and telephone wires. In such an event there would have been no means of giving prompt notice to Portland but by those beacon fires.

The war took a different turn, however, as the Germans who did the damage in Lyme Bay stayed out of sight and under the sea. There are six graves in St Michael's churchyard at Lyme Regis of sailors from the town's greatest offshore disaster of the conflict. From here you can look out across the waters where a German U-boat torpedoed the 15,000-ton battleship HMS *Formidable*, sailing last in line with the Fifth Battle Squadron from Portland Harbour. She was the first Naval casualty of the second year of the First World War, being torpedoed at 02.20 hours on New Year's Day, Friday 1 January 1915. Her position was 20 miles east of Start Point.

An orderly evacuation was carried out for two hours, as the battleship appeared to be stable, but at 04.39 she slipped under quite suddenly. Deteriorating weather had hampered the rescue operation. Of the crew of 780, only 233 were saved, some in their own cutter which had taken 20 hours to reach the shore at Lyme Regis. The Brixham trawler *Provident* carried out heroic rescues, as did the escort cruisers HMS *Topaze* and *Diamond*, which together brought a total of 80 survivors into Portland. For the remainder of the crew the sea became their grave.

U-boat *UB-24* was responsible, with two torpedoes from close range, and in the process only narrowly survived, having grazed the heaving keel of the warship. The ship's dog, an old terrier named Bruce, was also lost; he was last seen standing on duty beside his master, Captain Loxley, who remained with Commander Ballard on the bridge. Revd G. Brooke Robinson, formerly curate of Burton Bradstock and a prominent member of West Bay Swimming Club, was chaplain on board, and also went down with the ship. One of the ship's cutters, after being buffeted about in the gale for 20 hours, grounded on the beach in front of the Marine Parade, Lyme Regis, at about 22.45 on the Friday night. It was one of only two boats that got away from the wreck, the other being picked up by Captain Pillar's Brixham trawler, which he put about at the peril of his own life, in one of the worst south-easterly gales for years.

There were 50 men aboard the boat washed up at Lyme, but nine of them were dead or dying. Others had expired during the voyage, from injuries and exposure, and their bodies had been pushed overboard. At Lyme the press found another perfect 'Man's best friend' story.

John Cowen was the tenth body left for dead on the floor of the Pilot Boat Inn in Broad Street. During the night, however, the landlord's cross-bred collie started licking his face and hands. Charles Atkins' attention was drawn to his dog's agitation and a groan was heard to come from the body. From the jaws of disaster the press had their miracle to report:

Immediately willing hands completed the work the dog had begun and in a short time Cowen sat up. Since then the dog and Cowen have been inseparable, and as Cowen is not yet allowed out, he and the dog spend most of the time before the kitchen fire cultivating the acquaintance so curiously begun.

The loss of the *Formidable* raised questions, nationally, as the war that should have ended at Christmas edged towards stalemate. On 14 January 1915 the *Morning Post* demanded an official inquiry:

The Squadron was off Torbay. It was disposed in line ahead, that is, single file. The Formidable *was the last ship in the line. The weather was clear, the moon shining, the sea choppy but not very rough. German*

Final photograph of the battleship
HMS Formidable, *seen from HMS*
Agamemnon, *the evening before*
she was sunk by a German torpedo
off Lyme Regis.

Survivors photographed by Captain
G.C.C. Crookshank of HMS
Agamemnon – 'HMS Formidable.
Are We Downhearted? 1st Jan 1915.'

submarines were known to be in the Channel. In these circumstances the Squadron, disposed in line ahead, was steaming slowly. No conditions, except lying at anchor, could have been more favourable to attack by submarines.

The paper then explained that a single ship would sail on a zig-zag course to avoid torpedoes. In the case of a squadron of heavy ships the vessels followed their leader and their defence was left to escort vessels. These comprised 'a screen of destroyers, whose high speed and handiness afford a reasonable defence against submarines'.

The *Morning Post* established that such a screen had been lacking on New Year's Day and posed three questions that have never been adequately answered:

(1)   Why was the Squadron at sea at night?
(2)   Why was it deprived of its proper defence of destroyers?
(3)   Why was it steaming at slow speed?

Lyme's lifeboat had been unable to help. Launched on a service call just before Christmas, on 11 December 1914, she attempted to go to the aid of the Weymouth fishing boat the *Emma and John*. *Susan Ashley*, the Lyme lifeboat since 1891, made three attempts to break out through a ferocious sea that was piling in from the south and breaking across the entrance to the Cobb. The third attempt saw her smashed against the harbour wall. Then came the welcome news that the crew of the *Emma and John* had beached, east of the town, and walked ashore.

The *Susan Ashley* was sold for scrap in 1915, for £8.10s., and she was replaced by the 35-foot *Thomas Masterman Hardy* which was named for the 'kiss me Hardy' of Nelson's death on HMS *Victory*, who came from West Dorset and is commemorated by the Hardy Monument above Portesham. Built at East Cowes, Isle of Wight, this was one of the last dozen sailing lifeboats ever built.

West Dorset hosted the Howe Battalion, 2nd Royal Naval Brigade, of the Royal Naval Division, who arrived in January 1915 for an intensive course of training. Commanded by Lieutenant-Colonel C.G. Collins, they distinguished themselves during the hurried retreat from Antwerp, in October 1914, having marched 31 miles during one night to escape an encircling movement.

Nearly 1,000 men set to work on Eype Down, the big expanse of common land between Thorncombe Beacon and Symondsbury, practising trench-building with an elaborate series of zig-zagging entrenchments five to six feet deep. Snipers also trained, to ensure that the diggers kept their heads below ground level, and cooking was also carried out under service conditions. On Sundays they relaxed as hordes of people from the surrounding countryside came to view their efforts.

Few from the Howe Battalion would ever see Eype Down again. They were bound for the ill-fated landings in the Dardanelles and fell in the fighting at Gallipoli. Freedom of movement at home was less restricted than that under Turkish guns, but the National Registration Act saw everyone issued with a certificate, stating name, occupation, and postal address, which was to be carried whenever away from home, for presentation on demand.

A refugee from the war, to a Dorset country cottage at Fishpond Bottom on the southern slope of Lambert's Castle Hill, was the French 'impressionniste' painter Lucien Pissarro (1863–1944). The son of Camille Pissarro, he became a member of the New English Art Club and a naturalised British subject in 1916. Pissarro's summertime visitors included James Bolivar Manson

James Manson, friend of Lucien Pissarro, was another leading artist who adopted Lyme's countryside.

(1879–1944) of the Tate Gallery – then an assistant, rising to become its director in 1930 – who also had his own one-man exhibitions. They became close friends and took every opportunity for a stroll into the surrounding countryside to paint together.

By 1916, steel-wire submarine nets, manufactured in Bridport by Messrs W. Edwards & Son, were credited with having stopped an increasing number of enemy U-boats. Specially designed motor launches, based for a time at West Bay, also played havoc amongst them. Admiralty airships from Powerstock, floating gracefully over the English Channel, experimented with visual and electronic methods of locating submarines lurking in the water below, and swooped down to attack with depth-charge bombs.

Lyme Regis, on the other hand, became a laughing-stock for its spate of absurd U-boat alarms. One, which was actually reported to Scotland Yard, was that a German submarine base had been established in Pinhay Bay. It arose from the story:

... that a man was found unconscious on the rocks one day, who, when he came round, made the statement that while standing looking toward the land someone came up from behind and knocked him on the head.

A German sailor, from under the sea, became the popular explanation.

'Road from the hill, Fishpond', by Lucien
Pissarro, shows Lyme's hinterland from
the south-east slopes of Lambert's Castle.

'A Dorset garden' by Lucien Pissarro.

Town view from the Spittles between the wars.

Similarly, an elderly lady visitor to Lyme, seeing a man around the same rocks each day, assumed he was sending wireless messages to U-boats; he was found to be picking limpets. Another man was accused of taking money for supplying petrol to German agents. Closer observation revealed it to be Samuel Curtis, fishmonger and fossil hunter, selling his wares.

The 3,073-ton freighter *Baygitano* was torpedoed by German submarine *U-77*, inshore in Lyme Bay on 18 March 1918, only a mile-and-a-half south-west of Lyme Regis. Two of the crew were drowned but the remainder were safely taken off by the town's lifeboat and other small craft which came to the rescue of the sinking steamship. Built in 1903 and owned by the Bay Steam Ship Company, she was in ballast and returning from Le Havre to Cardiff, having delivered a cargo of coal. She is now known in Lyme as 'The Wreck'.

The *Moidart*, an 1878-built collier of 1,303 tons, was torpedoed and sunk seven miles south-east of Lyme Regis by German submarine UC-77 on 9 June 1918. She was carrying a cargo of coal up-Channel from Barry, South Wales. Her crew of 15 were lost.

West Dorset had its heroes among the tragedies. As an example for the whole of the war, there were the exploits of Captain John Glossop, who retired as Vice-Admiral John Collings Taswell Glossop (1871–1934) to Bothenhampton. He commanded the cruiser HMAS *Sydney* when she sank the German

raider *Emden* in the Indian Ocean on 9 November 1914. He might have emerged with more credit were it not for a swashbuckling party of 49 Germans under Kapitanleutnant Helmuth von Mucke who achieved an all-time long-distance escape record. Having landed from the *Emden* on British-owned Direction Island in the Cocos Keeling group off Western Australia, 42 of them made it safely home to the other side of the globe. They reported back for duty nearly six months later.

Commander Victor Crutchley (1893–1986) of Mappercombe Manor, Nettlecombe, near Powerstock, was awarded the Victoria Cross and the French Croix de Guerre for his audacious second and successful attempt at blocking Ostend Harbour in the spring of 1918. Admiral Sir Victor Crutchley, as he became, remained at sea between the wars and commanded the 30,600-ton battleship HMS *Warspite* from 1937 to 1940. After a spell ashore as the Commodore at Devonport he returned to the water to command the Australian Naval Squadron, 1942–44. He was then Flag Officer Gibraltar until retirement in 1947. On land, to mention just one local hero, Captain Julian Royds Gribble (1897–1918) of Kingston Russell was mortally wounded while fighting with the Royal Warwicks. He was posthumously awarded the Victoria Cross.

The first news of the Armistice to reach West Dorset came by wireless to the Royal Naval Airship Station at Powerstock, at 06.30 hours in the morning of 11 November 1918, straight from Paris, stating that hostilities would cease at 11 o'clock. The message was passed on to the Flag Officer at Portland, who confirmed its authenticity with the Admiralty. He issued the following signal by telegraph at 07.45 hours. A contemporary copy is with me as I write and I shall re-type it as received. This is from form S.-1320b, transcribed verbatim, with 'AAA' being code for a full stop followed by a new line:

Naval Signal.
From Flag Officer, Portland.
Telegraph to All Units, R.N. and R.M., Portland Command Area
Hostilities will cease at 1100 hrs to-day Nov 11th AAA
All precautions to be preserved and there will be no communication with the Enemy AAA
All units are to report dispositions and to remain at

a state of readiness to meet any demand AAA
Further instructions will be issued regarding enemy units, especially submarines, now at sea AAA
Acknowledge AAA

By eight o'clock, starting with the bells of St Mary at Bridport, joyous peals rang out across West Dorset.

Major F.C. Butler and his brother, on returning home from the war, set about mobilising West Dorset with its first regular motor bus service. This ran to Lyme Regis, from Axminster Station, in February 1920. Butler Bros then began a service from Bridport to Lyme from Whitsun in 1921. National Buses, later regionalised as Southern National, introduced a service from West Bay to Axminster, via Lyme Regis, in July 1922. The motorised age had at last arrived, although on the land it would take another half-century for the tractor to put an end to horse plough-ing in the rustic backwaters of the Marshwood Vale.

The War Memorial, with nearly 100 names from two great twentieth-century conflicts,
representing a higher than usual toll for a population of around 3,000.

Broad Street down from Fox and Son (right) *to the Three Cups Hotel* (centre) *with the Royal Lion Hotel opposite* (left) *in 1910.*

Broad Street in 1920, uphill from the cart of bakers Clifford Sanders and Sons (right), *and the New Commercial Inn and Royal Lion Hotel.*

Fishing boat on a sultry day.

Portrait of 'An old inhabitant' on a postcard posted from Lyme in 1927.

Above: *Steamer reversing out of the Cobb
beside the central breakwater in 1913.*

Right: *Timeless survival, in an Edwardian watercolour
by Raphael Tuck in 1902, with Charmouth's cliffs
as the backdrop to the Cobb entrance.*

Horse mowing of a meadow at Lyme, beneath huge elm trees, in 1925.

Above: *Fishermen, coastguard, sailor and visitors on the Cobb approach in 1905.*

Cottages fronting the Forge in Broad Street with Fanny Adams being the lady in black (right) *in the 1880s.*

The Town Hall and Gun Cliff in 1920.

Church Street and what was then the White Hart Inn in a late Victorian view.

Looking westwards up Pound Street in 1912.

The Royal Lion Hotel and New Inn in a view down Broad Street in 1919.

A combination of sodden clay and a lively sea carried off a section of Marine Parade on 5 December 1926.

*The first
Lyme-owned
car with
Richard Wallace
giving Spike Hardy
a ride in his
De Dion Buton, 1902.*

*Motor cars climbing out of Lyme were still a rarity in 1911, warranting a photo-call
for the residents of Turnpike Cottage.*

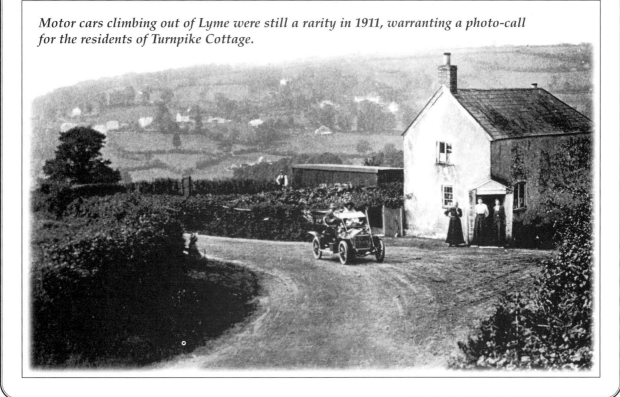

Cemetery and its mortuary chapels, looking north-westwards towards Charmouth Road in 1997.

The Buddle from the sea, as it looked during the middle of the twentieth century.

Chapter 11

NEILL, JELLICOE, FOWLES & WHISTLER II

Acclaimed or notorious after it left Lyme Regis, depending on your point of view, the progressive 'do as you please' Summerhill School was established by Alexander Sutherland Neill (1883–1973) in the house called Summerhill in Charmouth Road. Neill progressed from office boy to draper before turning teacher and psychologist in 1924. His philosophy was explained in books such as *The Problem Child*, *The Problem Parent*, *The Problem Teacher* and *The Problem Family* with his solution being *The Free Child*. Summerhill School moved on to Leiston in Suffolk and the house on the hill became Summerhill Private Hotel (proprietress Mrs T.G. Miles).

Royal doctor Sir Maurice Abbot-Anderson (1861–1938) retired to Madeira Cottage on Marine Parade – which was still being called the Walk – in 1928. He was physician to the Princess Royal, Louise, Duchess of Fife, and had founded Flora's League to campaign for the conservation of wild flowers. When he extended his thatched home, putting a miniature look-alike cottage next to it, he did the work so well that the Royal Commission on Historical Monuments listed it as an ancient building. In the process he also illegally stopped-up a public footpath.

His widow, Lady Muriel Abbot-Anderson (1888–1973), carried on with Flora's League until after the Second World War. She was buried with Sir Maurice in Lyme cemetery but no inscription was added to record the fact. What would have pleased the pair was that by the 1980s the area had become carpeted with the daffodils that Lady Muriel had planted. They would have been less happy that the existence and purpose of Flora's League were forgotten after it merged with the Council for the Preservation of Rural England. This is now the Council for the Protection of Rural England whose spokesman was unaware of the connection.

Lyme can also claim an enigmatic link – said with flowers – with the greatest old-style warrior hero of the twentieth century. The sole floral tribute, of lilac and forget-me-nots, at the burial of Lawrence of Arabia in Moreton cemetery on 21 May 1935, carried a Lyme Regis hotel label with the message: 'To T.E.L. who should sleep among Kings.'

Winston Churchill led the mourners and expressed sadness that Lawrence had been lost to the nation, in an inexplicable motorcycle accident, at a time when the coming conflict would have found him in new roles. Lyme Regis and Dorset would soon be on the front line once again. In August 1939 the Lyme Regis Bombing Range, covering 16 square miles of sea, was designated by the Air Ministry for daylight use. An initial limit of 120lb was imposed on live bombs that could be dropped.

Prime Minister Neville Chamberlain announced the declaration of war against Germany in a Sunday morning broadcast from the Cabinet Room in No. 10 Downing Street. Two days later, on 5 September 1939, in Tuesday's *K Destroyer Flotilla News*, the daily newspaper of the 5th Destroyer Flotilla, Bob Knight reported to the crew of HMS *Kelly* on the fishy sequel resulting from anti-submarine depth-charges which had claimed a U-boat in Lyme Bay on Monday:

That's war – that was; but we must not lead ourselves to believe that some of the catch will always appear on the breakfast table. The presence of mind of Posty in producing a gaff to lift the whales inboard while the ship had stopped to obtain a sample of the oil on the sea is much to be admired. We all hope that the Kelly's *and* Acheron's *efforts* [another destroyer] *did away with one of the pests that sank, without warning, the liner* Athenia *on Sunday night* [3 September, off Ireland] *– and, of course, we hope that the lucky messes in the* Kelly *enjoyed their breakfast.*

There is plenty of corroborative evidence to show that there were two U-boats here yesterday, one in Weymouth Bay and one in West Bay. The periscope of the former was seen from the signal bridge of the Resolution *and the M.A.S.B. and the tracks of two torpedoes fired at the* Kelly. *They missed us by 30 or 40 yards, so certainly we were lucky. To be missed by one submarine and bag another* [later, in Lyme Bay] *all in the first day* [at sea, from Portland] *is good going.*

The following year the Royal Navy's losses mounted. On 12 April 1940 a laurel wreath was placed on the door of the Hardy Monument, the memorial to Nelson's flag captain on the hills above Portesham – the village known to Thomas Hardy as 'Possum' – in memory of the men of the Royal Navy who lost their lives two days previously in Narvik fjord, Norway. A card read:

To the unfading memory of Captain Warburton-Lee, RN, HMS Hardy, *and the gallant men who died at Narvik. Nelson's Hardy and Hardy's Possum salute you.*

On land, the 3rd Infantry Division camped around Lyme Regis in 1939 and the East Surrey, Suffolk and Middlesex Regiments were assigned to construction and manning of its anti-invasion defences. Dragon's-teeth anti-tank traps were constructed with great cubes of concrete, pillboxes were built, and beaches obstructed and mined.

Overhead, from the start of the Battle of Britain in July 1940, the air defence of Lyme Bay was shared between Spitfires from RAF Warmwell to the east and Hurricanes from RAF Exeter to the west. The latter were particularly hard-pressed, and had least chance of seeing reinforcements from aerodromes further inland, with 15 August 1940 in particular proving to be the most spectacular and costly flying display ever seen from the West Dorset cliffs.

Twenty-seven-year-old Squadron Leader Terence Lovell-Gregg of 87 Squadron, from RAF Exeter, failed in a desperate attempt to make a crash landing in the Fleet lagoon late in the afternoon. The Hurricane came in blazing over the sea but was brought into a controlled descent for a forced landing. P3215 then clipped a tree beside Abbotsbury Swannery and its wounded pilot fell to his death.

Flying Officer Roland Prosper Beamont, one of the Exeter pilots, returned with the story of how Lovell-Gregg had led his squadron into the midst of a mass of German aircraft at 18,000 feet over the English Channel:

We saw the 'Beehive' almost straight ahead at the same height, and with his Hurricanes, Lovell-Gregg flew straight at the centre of the formation without hesitation or deviation in any way.

A total of 120 enemy aircraft were heading towards Portland. Lovell-Gregg was a quiet pre-war professional, from Marlborough in New Zealand, who had taught many of the emergent generation of flyers. His courage was never in any doubt, although he had led his squadron for only a month, since 12 July. The pilots knew him as 'Shovel'. There were only four of them with him when they scrambled at 16.00 hours. Five Hurricanes were all the air-worthy machines that 87 Squadron could muster. Undaunted by the adverse odds of fifteen-to-one that loomed in front, Lovell-Gregg asked the impossible of his men. His last words of encouragement, Beamont said, were characteristically defiant: 'Come on chaps, let's surround them!'

Those fortunate enough to bale out in such situations stood a chance of being picked up by No. 37 Air Sea Rescue Unit of the Royal Air Force which was based at the Cobb. It also policed the bombing range and saved a couple of dozen ditched British aircrew plus three German flyers. It also arrived in the nick of time for a Horsa glider, being towed with men of the Devonshire Regiment practising paratroop techniques, saving all but one of the 28 soldiers and crew. In all 65 men stepped to safety at Lyme Regis from launches during the Second World War. The unit, with *Launch 1644* being its familiar vessel carrying the reassuring roundels, continued to operate from Lyme into the Cold War, until 1964.

The most worrying time for Lyme's defenders during the war came on 7 September 1940 when it appeared that the long-awaited German invasion had started. Reports had been received of a seven-mile convoy heading towards the Dorset coast and there was 'a general flap on' that Operation Sealion was taking place and Field-Marshal Fedor von Bock was on his way with the victors of Poland, the Wehrmacht's Army Group B. Eastwards, the fuel tanks were to be fired to set beaches ablaze, and an aircraft from Gosport dropped incendiaries to start them off. Troops at Bournemouth who manned the cliffs kept emphasising that 'this is not an exercise'.

At 20.07 hours a national alert was issued by the War Office: 'Condition Cromwell'. An invasion was regarded as 'imminent and probable' within 12 hours. Nothing happened, however, but invasion fears reached fever pitch. This was not entirely without reason, for aerial reconnaissances were showing concentrations of ships and barges along the French coast, from Brest to Calais.

German mines were a particular peril in Lyme Bay. The British armed trawler HMT *Lord Stamp* sank after striking a mine on 14 October 1940 (HMT was the abbreviation for His Majesty's Trawler). Three days later the Royal Navy's losses of armed trawlers to the German minefield off West Dorset continued when HMT *Kingston Cairngorm* blew up near Portland Bill.

From overseas, on 27 March 1941, news reached the town that Wing Commander Edward Collis de Virac Lart (1902–41) of Lyme Regis, whose flying career began in the 1920s with 60 (Bombing) Squadron in India, was missing, presumed dead, on failing to return to his base. The town fought back with cash as well as manpower, it being announced in June 1941 that Lyme Regis had contributed £69,222 in war savings 'towards sending another ship to fight in His Majesty's Navy for the freedom of mankind from the Nazi thrall.' This was £25.10s. per head from the 2,700 inhabitants. Champion Town Crier Walter Abbott made the announcement of 'this Empire's determination to guard our rightful place on the good Earth.'

Ship Number 582, a Royal Navy warship that had been ordered as HMS *Sunderland*, was re-named HMS *Lyme Regis* on being launched into the River Clyde on 19 March 1942. Built by Alexander Stephens & Sons Ltd, at Linthouse Yard, Govan, she was a 650-ton Bangor-class minesweeper. On completion, on 2 June 1942, she sailed for sea trials off Tobermory and achieved an acceptable maximum speed of 15.5 knots. Working-up was followed by assignment to the 15th Minesweeping Flotilla, at Aultbea, on Loch Ewe.

Back on the Dorset coast, the occupants of an RAF coastal radar station at Cain's Folly, on the cliffs east of Charmouth, had a shock from an older enemy on 14 May 1942. The ground had literally opened up beneath them. A landslip carried away concrete buildings and deposited them on the tumbled under-cliff some 50 feet below.

The task of the RAF contingent on the cliff was to scan the sea as well as the air. Thursday 9 July 1942 turned into what is known as the Battle of Lyme Bay. It was an audacious attack carried out by the German 1st Schnellboot Flotilla (S48, S50, S63, S67, S70, S104, S109) against Allied coast Convoy EP-91. A total of 12,192 tons of shipping was sunk – the tanker SS *Pomella* and four freighters. One of the British escorts was also lost, HMT *Manor*, an armed trawler.

Lyme's own warship kept up with the progress of the war, coming in sight of the Atlas Mountains and Sahara Desert when she escorted Convoy KMS-4 to Gibraltar in December 1942, after the Operation Torch landings in Algiers, Oran and Casablanca. HMS *Lyme Regis*, with HMS *Whitehaven* as Flotilla Leader, then returned to Britain with Convoy MKS-3X. In January 1943 she repeated the sequence with Convoy KMS-7 outward bound and MKS-6 on the homeward run.

On 15 February 1943, the crew of HMS *Lyme Regis* found themselves facing climatic challenges, with a northern turn out of Loch Ewe as Convoy JW-53 headed for Iceland and Russia. Tanks and railway locomotives were tied to the decks of some of the 25 merchant ships. This was one of the famous runs commanded by Commodore Ernest Leir from Ditcheat in Somerset. They were about to be ambushed, but by the weather rather than the Germans.

A gale off the Butt of Lewis took a tin-opener to the cruiser HMS *Sheffield*. Veterans who had survived the friendly fire of Swordfish torpedoes (from pilots told they were bearing down on the Bismarck) were amazed to see the top of the forward gun turret rolled back by waves which covered the entire ship. A Naval correspondent kept *Dorset County Chronicle* readers abreast of other shocks to the system in the 200-mile gap between Norway and the Germans, and the ice-sheets of the Arctic:

The cold dawn came out of the east, to discover the bridges, and exposed portions of all ships, thickly covered in frozen snow. Hot cocoa arrived on the bridge, while once more we steamed around the convoy, chasing up a laggard, and shouting at one ship with an extra turn of speed to drop back into her proper station.

Back in Lyme Bay, for four days at the end of February 1943, the 5th Schnellboot Flotilla harried a Channel convoy. The action moved slowly up-Channel to Portland and the Isle of Wight. Two of the escorts protecting Convoy CHA-172, the armed trawlers HMT *Harstad* and HMT *Lord Hailsham*, were sunk. The freighter *Moldavia*, 4,858 tons, was also lost, together with a new 658-ton tank landing-craft, LCT381.

My favourite anecdote from wartime Lyme comes from the *Daily Telegraph* of 31 August 1943. The diary column reported that a Lyme Regis hotelier had received a stamped addressed postcard from an anxious prospective visitor asking for 'the date of the last enemy attack on your town'. The manager sent the card back with the date – '1685'.

There had in fact been a bomb that hit the town. It was apparently dropped by a Heinkel bomber returning to France after a raid on Bristol. The explo-sion took off the roof of Woolcombe Cottage which was the home of Frances and Richard Hutchings. Their daughter, Lucy, had a narrow escape as the windows blew out and shrapnel peppered the bedroom wall. Immediately above her head, nine small pieces of metal tore through a framed painting. The damaged painting, a watercolour of an old stone-roofed cottage, still hangs in Woolcombe Cottage which is now the home of David and Wendy Cannings. For a time the picture was the property of former 'world champion Town Crier' Richard Fox, but he gave it back to Mr and Mrs Cannings as a Christmas present in 2001: 'I thought it was impor-tant to have it preserved and back in the same place as a record of the only bomb that fell on Lyme Regis in the war.'

Cannon fire also sprayed the London Inn, reputedly scoring treble 20 on the dartboard, as the enemy aircraft was engaged by Hurricane fighters from RAF Exeter. They shot it down into Lyme Bay. Local fisherman John Wason dredged up three of its propeller blades in 1974.

As tens of thousands of American soldiers poured into Dorset during the winter of 1943, with equip-ment and stores that covered hundreds of acres, Lyme found itself hosting the 16th Infantry Regiment of the United States 1st Infantry Division. Tented camps sprang up around the town. On 16 April 1944 there was a major move on the ground of forces preparing for the invasion of Normandy.

None, other than those privy to the 'Bigot' secret as it was code-named, were aware that the invasion of Hitler's Europe was to come from the Dorset coast. Officially-released disinformation and rumours implied that all this was merely a feint and, as Hitler himself wanted to believe, the actual assault would be made from 'Caesar's Coast' of Sussex and Kent, across to the Seine and Calais. Even the actual arrangements were still in a degree of turmoil.

Although expected to gather in Portland and Weymouth for Operation Overlord, British invasion Force G was relocated eastwards to the harbours and inlets of the Solent and Southampton Water. Instead the Dorset ports were allocated to United States Force O. They were destined for what is designated as Omaha Beach and the British troops were to land in the next sector to the east, code-named Gold Beach. Captain J.J. McGlynn of the United States Navy took up his post as Commanding Officer United States Navy Advanced Amphibious Base Portland and Weymouth. This included the three hards at Portland and HMS *Grasshopper*, the Royal Navy shore base at Weymouth, plus ancillary facilities.

Captain McGlynn was to be responsible for the embarkation of V Corps of the First United States Army which comprised the 1st US Infantry Division, 2nd US Infantry Division, 2nd US Armored Division, and two Ranger battalions. Lyme's Americans were from the 'Fighting Firsts' or 'Big Red One', as America's famous First Infantry Division is known to this day, and had their Divisional Headquarters at Langton House, near Blandford. The Commanding General, Major-General Clarence R. Huebner, had at his command 34,142 men and 3,306 vehicles. It was estimated that there were a total of 80,000 American soldiers who are billeted in Dorset, from the tents at Lyme and chalets of Freshwater holiday camp on the coast at Burton Bradstock to the grounds of Charborough Park and Nissen huts in hazel coppices on Cranborne Chase.

Offshore in Lyme Bay, disaster threatened to unhinge the plans on 28 April 1944. Convoy T-4, comprising eight American tank landing ships (known as LSTs for Landing Ship Tanks), was making a circuit of the bay during Exercise Tiger, preparing for practice landings at Slapton Sands, when they were intercepted by E-boats in the English Channel at 02.50 hours.

Motor torpedo boats of the 5th and 9th Schnellboot Flotillas ran amok amongst the Americans south-west of Portland Bay. A total of 441 United States soldiers were killed or drowned, together with 197 seamen, with the sinking of *LST507* and *LST531*. What was described as a 'handful' of Royal Artillery anti-aircraft Bofors gunners were also killed and an unknown number of men injured. Twelve tanks were also lost and a third ship, *LST289*, was damaged by a torpedo and limped westwards to Dartmouth. *LST511* was raked by gunfire and escaped the other way, around Portland Bill, into Weymouth Bay. Coastal gun batteries, at Blacknor Fort on Portland, prepared to open fire but were ordered not to do so by the American commander, in view of the number of his men who were in the water.

The only protection for the LSTs was a single Flower-class corvette, HMS *Azalea*, of 925 tons and just two guns, and the closest other Allied warship at sea at the time was 15 miles away. She was the 1918-built destroyer HMS *Saladin* which would be followed to the scene by a modern destroyer, HMS *Onslow*, built in 1941.

HMS *Scimitar*, a 1919-built destroyer of 905 tons, had been assigned to join HMS *Azalea* to escort Convoy T-4 but was withdrawn to Portland Naval Base the previous morning due to slight damage to the bows arising from a collision with a LCI (Landing Craft Infantry) which occurred the night before, in Tor Bay. Six MTBs of the 63rd Motor Torpedo Boat Flotilla were also in Portland Bay, having just returned from patrols into enemy-occupied French waters. Their crews were woken by alarms but could not make any sense of radio messages, one of them told me: 'There was a fair amount of w/t (wireless telegraphy) traffic but it was all in code; a code that Coastal Forces boats were not issued with.'

The remainder of the story I have documented in *Wartime Dorset*. It had been accumulated over the years, feeling through what was an inevitable veil of secrecy that was never subsequently lifted. The dead were stacked in piles on Castletown Pier at Portland and Navy divers worked for days to account for every identity disc. Survivors were dispersed to various military hospitals along the South Coast. Medical staff were briefed not to inquire into the circumstances of their injuries. The consequences would have been court martials.

There was sensitivity that the instructions of the Supreme Allied Commander, General Dwight D. Eisenhower, had been ignored and that Bigot-classified personnel – those knowing the D-Day secrets – had been put in a position where they might have been captured and interrogated by the Germans. Fortunately, Allied Naval Headquarters could offer some solace, that they were dead rather than rescued by the enemy: 'This cloud's silver lining is that the invasion plans remain safe and secure.'

Off Normandy, hours ahead of D-Day, 'Action stations' sounded on HMS *Lyme Regis* on the afternoon of 5 June 1944, when she found herself in the vanguard of Operation Neptune in preparing the way for the biggest armada in history. She was sent with four Canadian minesweepers, HMCS *Gainsborough*, HMCS *Georgian*, HMCS *Kenova* and HMCS *Versailles*, to clear a channel west of the Seine estuary for the approach of British assault Force S, for Sword, which was tasked to land at dawn on Sword Beach. Flotilla Leader HMS *Fraserburgh* was hit overnight by a mine or a bomb, forcing her to depart for Portsmouth, and HMS *Lyme Regis* was promoted in her place. 'Battle Honours' were awarded to *Lyme Regis* for her work in enabling assault troops and then the Allied-land force commander, General Sir Bernard Montgomery, to land in Normandy.

Dorset's Americans were the heroes of 'Bloody Omaha', the scene of the worst Allied casualties of the D-Day invasion. They lost 3,000 lives on D-Day before their beachhead objectives were eventually secured as dusk dropped on this longest day. Total losses in the Battle of Normandy would be 37,000 Allied dead, and 58,000 German fatalities.

For HMS *Lyme Regis* the war went westwards, to clear Cherbourg Harbour, before she could follow the advance into the Reich. Her war ended in the final contested triangle of sea between Harwich, Flushing and the Friesian Islands. VE day was celebrated in Bridlington Bay with a shuttle service of ferries bringing the town to the ship. Postwar, there were mines to find and wrecks to clear along the North Sea coast, followed by retirement into the Reserve Fleet at Milford Haven. Short-term secondment for target practice was followed by her sale for scrap in 1948. She was towed from Plymouth to Sunderland – her original name, when she was laid down in 1941 – where she was cut up by C.W. Dorkin & Company in the North Dock.

Meanwhile, on her home coast, mines had to be cleared in their thousands. On 4 August 1947, Major A.B. Hartley of Southern Command announced that the 16th and 17th Bomb Disposal Squads of the Royal Engineers had so far disposed of 9,000 anti-invasion mines near Weymouth. This included a total of some 3,200 from a mile of shingle beach and clayey cliffs at Ringstead Bay. Those operations, which still had to be completed eastwards into Purbeck, had so far cost the lives of three officers and 22 other ranks. One officer had been blinded.

Life in Lyme had already returned to something like normality with the film 'All Over the Town' being completed there in 1948, under the guise of Tormouth.

In 1962 there was an echo of Sedgemoor and Lyme's ill-fated rebellion of 1685. A skull, thought to be that of James Scott, the Duke of Monmouth, was discovered under No. 10 Downing Street during an excavation by Ministry of Works archaeologist Michael Green, it was reported on 8 March. It was found in a container that had been hewn from a single piece of stone that was just long enough to hold it.

Forensic scientists said the head was of a man in his 30s executed at least 250 years ago, hit by a blunt axe on the forehead and with a mass of cuts on the back of the neck. The Duke's axing is known to have been bungled; he was struck five times and the execution had to be finished off with a knife. He had lodgings in Whitehall Palace, on the Treasury site, and the place where the skull was found may have been his garden. A further clue was that the skull had been exposed for a time, as would have been the custom. Although some remains of the Duke were found in Victorian times in the chapel of St Peter and Vincula in the Tower of London these do not appear to have included the head. Monmouth, the illegitimate son of Charles II, was beheaded at the age of 36, after his landing at Lyme Regis and defeat on the battlefield of Sedgemoor, in the abortive Western Rebellion against his uncle James II in 1685.

Discovery of the skull coincided with momentous events above Monmouth Beach. Ominous cracks

Deck-chairs and 1950s fashions on Marine Parade, towards the eastern end.

Looking down Broad Street in the 1950s from Love & Sons butchers (left)
and the Volunteers Arms and Wool Shop (right).

Broad Street, down from the Midland Bank (right) *and alleyway to the Holmcroft Hotel, in 1965.*

and rumblings in 1962 were the precursor of one of the worst landslips for years. Houses juddered, with some leaning alarmingly, as thousands of tons of clay and rock cascaded across Marine Parade. The earthquake was exacerbated by an ill-advised house-building project in the most unstable part of the town. What was initially seen as a disaster also turned into an opportunity, which was subsequently realised by the extension of Langmoor Gardens, with the additional section above the Cobb being named the Lord Lister Gardens in memory of the pioneer of antiseptic surgery.

Playwright Ann Jellicoe (born 1927) of Colway Manor, Colway Lane, came to fame with *The Knack* which in both content and timing – published in 1961 as a book and turned into a lively film in 1965 – spearheaded pop culture in the 'Swinging Sixties'. She then took drama backwards in unique time-capsules to the Duke of Monmouth's 1685 rebellion, with one-off performances by Colway Theatre Trust that starred descendants of his vanquished peasant army. Other regional offerings found wider audiences through South West Arts. Ann Jellicoe's second marriage, in 1962, was to photographer Roger Mayne whose iconic black-and-white images captured streetwise realities of contemporary urban life.

What Ann Jellicoe did for popular culture, John Fowles (born 31 March 1926) achieved for the English novel and Lyme's international fame, after arriving at Underhill Farm in the 1960s. He was born in Essex and evacuated from London to Devon in 1939. John Fowles and wife Elizabeth Whitton soon moved on to Belmont House, Eleanor Coade's home above the Cobb, having been jolted into this when a couple of adjoining fields beside Undercliff National Nature Reserve slid towards the sea. With the build of Orson Welles and beard of Alexander Solzhenytzin Fowles was already a cult figure. *The Collector*, in 1963, was ahead of its time. A lepidopterist comes into money, buys a van, and uses his chloroform bottle to capture a girl instead. It was followed by the deep novel *Aristos* in 1965, and surreal psychology in *The Magus* in 1966, for which he proceeded to rewrite a 'post-parental' erotic version ending with a couple of lines of verse in Latin. 'One of the most obdurately literary men of our time,' Anthony Burgess called him. 'It remains a badly written book,' Fowles mused, 'but I have great affection for it.'

The Collector and *The Magus* had already been made into films but his wider fame followed in the wake of *The French Lieutenant's Woman*. Set in the town, and on the landslipped undercliff around his home, it won immediate national acclaim as the most important Dorset novel since Thomas Hardy's *Tess of the d'Urbervilles*. Fowles' social outcast is Sarah Woodruff. Her locations and period – the Napoleonic Wars – were Hardyescue but the book went further, closing its Victorian format midway, and extending beyond its era with the hindsight of the world of Darwin, Engels and Marx. It also advanced the methodology of the novel. Having almost ended it once, in the middle, the author steps in to give it a

Chimney Rock (left) *and Underhill Farm* (right) *at the eastern end of the Landslip, in 1904, which became John Fowles' first home in Lyme.*

Lyme author John Fowles on the upper terrace beside Belmont House.

Inset: *John Fowles as museum curator explaining the purpose of a smugglers' weight for sinking kegs.*

The author, John Fowles.

Bamboo forest, hiding the author's slopes from Stile Lane, between Belmont and Langmoor Gardens.

choice of two final endings. In one, fossil collector Charles proposes marriage to Sarah, and is accepted. In the alternative she rejects him. 'It is like a sexual experience,' the author explained. 'Just as you never want a satisfying love affair to end, so it is with a novel.'

Praised by his peers, with Malcolm Bradbury describing it as 'the best book out of Britain in the 1960s', it won literary prizes. He coined the phrase 'Character Liberation' for the way in which the characters were set free of the plot 'having grown beyond him, and us'. The *French Lieutenant's Woman* was published in translation around the globe. More importantly, for the sake of Lyme and its tourist trade, Karel Reisz's film of the novel utilised the dramatic Lyme landscapes. A storm-lashed Cobb, endangering the leading lady, contrasted with the romantic setting of wild garlic in the leaf litter of the Undercliff for the lovers' tryst played by Jeremy Irons and Meryl Streep.

He went on to write *The Ebony Tower*, *Daniel Martin* and *A Maggot*. The latter concerns the disappearance, while travelling on horseback, of two men and their male servants and a maid. A month later the corpse of one of the servants, a deaf mute called Dick, is found hanged with a posy of violets stuffed in his mouth. The novel received a particularly entertaining review in the *Daily Express* in September 1985:

In page after page of question and answer testimony, an extraordinary tale unfolds of strange scientific quests, witchcraft and dark ceremonies in which another of the travellers has died as well as the unfortunate Dick. Could I believe all this? No. Was I puzzled? Yes. Was I entertained? Intermittently, especially by the odder fruits of Mr Fowles's erudition. Did you know that no Englishwoman until the 1790s wore any underclothes beneath her petticoat? Even the most elegant, like the Gainsborough lady were 'to put it brutally, knicker-less'.

This remarkable erudition was also put to academic use. From 1979 to 1982, John Fowles collaborated with me in transcribing and publishing John Aubrey's antiquarian magnum opus *Monumenta Britannica* which had lain in manuscript in the Bodleian Library for nearly three centuries. He regarded the puzzling jumble of language and locations that I sent him each day as the brain-teasing alternative to a crossword. His pride and joy, gradually returning to nature, was the biggest garden in Lyme Regis, rising from a dense bamboo forest beside Stile Path to herb-rich turf with exotic plants from cuttings and seeds he had pocketed on visits to great parks the world over. 'Belmont Botanical Garden,' I used to call it.

John Fowles' wife of 33 years, Elizabeth, died in 1990. Having received an honorary degree from the University of East Anglia, he married Sarah in 1998,

The classic Fowles setting, where Meryl Streep stood in salt spray, looking eastwards over the Cobb breakwater to Golden Cap and Thorncombe Beacon (centre).

and established the John Fowles Literary Trust. Run by a committee of academics headed by Professor Chris Bigsby, it will eventually manage Belmont House and its sprawling grounds as a retreat for writers from all over the world:

I have enjoyed living here so much and just would like, before I go, to feel that I have left something to help liter-ature, not simply the academic side. I've got an idea of a college, not quite what you normally think of as a college, but more a place where writers could come and stay, mix a little and get to know each other. It would be run under the aegis of Chris Bigsby's university and various other universities.

Lyme's second Whistler was rising to the top of his chosen art form. While living at Little Place in Lyme Regis in the 1960s and '70s, glass engraver Sir Laurence Whistler (1912–2000) worked on the windows for St Nicholas's Parish Church at Moreton, between Dorchester and Wareham. The dainty Georgian building had been blown apart by a German bomb in 1940, which presented him with the opportunity of working on every window in the church. Starting in 1955, and finishing three decades later, he had made Moreton unique in having the only church in the world with entirely engraved glass windows. The remarkable thing that strikes a visitor is how light and airy it makes the building – unlike the heavy effect of traditional stained glass – although Sir Laurence told me that his work showed up best against a black background. This showed his lines as white marks, bringing out the full power of his exuberant style, climaxing at Moreton in the swirling stars of spiralling galaxies over the west door.

While at Lyme both his style and methods developed apace. He had already moved on from etching with acid, or using an engraving wheel, to a

diamond point. Then he adopted a carbon-tipped dentist's drill and reserved the diamond for the finest of finishing touches. What marred the Moreton achievement was a 'ridiculous theological fuss' over the thirteenth and last window. The tiny pane, 'a blind window, looking nowhere', featured Judas Iscariot. As much as anything, Sir Laurence was upset that 'silly ignorant people' had questioned his artistry, rather than having focused on the fear that 'I had turned into a Christian subversive who was creating the church of Saint Judas.'

At such times he found writing cathartic, as he had after 'the two really special people' of his life had died in tragic circumstances. He lost his wife, actress Jill Furse, after she gave birth to their daughter in 1944. *The Initials in the Heart* he called her biography. The other loss that year was his elder brother, portrait and mural painter Rex Whistler (1905–44), who was killed in Normandy. Laurence Whistler had started his career as a poet and received a gold medal from King George V when *Four Walls* was chosen as the best volume of verse published in England in 1934. He was knighted in the millennium New Year honours and died on 19 December 2000.

Sir Laurence Whistler of Little Place at Lyme who turned glass engraving into a new art form.

Moreton Church, bombed in 1940, provided the opportunity for Whistler's life-long work.

Whistler's medium began with magic scratches in this Georgian apse and progressed to every window in St Nicholas's Parish Church at Moreton.

Laurence Whistler's style evolved into a celebration of light, as symbolised by these candles.

High tide in the Cobb harbour, in 1905, looking north-eastwards to Charmouth.

Regatta day at the Cobb in 1959.

Chapter 12
SEA DRAMAS & RINGING CHANGES

The Watts family from Bournemouth, beside beach tents below Marine Parade in 1922.

There was something of an interregnum between the departure of RAF Air Sea Rescue craft and the reinstatement of the Lyme lifeboat by the Royal National Lifeboat Institution. Not that the sea refrained from hostilities, such as on 23 June 1966 when trawler-man Ron Gollop and a speedboat proprietor went into action to save four people in difficulties in a dingy. In August 1966 two people were taken off *Toni*, a yacht, which was taken in tow off Black Ven. Here there were rumblings on land with dramatic repercussions on the shoreline.

Britain's most active landslip was on the move once again, from 477 feet on the cliffs west of Charmouth, down through the entire Black Ven undercliff. It became a treacherous mud flow which

was impossible to cross. Having overwhelmed the beach, in 1969, it slid 200 yards out to sea with a spit that projected across the Canary Ledges.

What Ron Gollop achieved at sea, Ken Gollop was matching on land, 'doing the rounds of fund-raising and letter writing' with W.L. Heape to persuade the Royal National Lifeboat Institution to reinstate Lyme to station status. Wing Commander F.A. Buckingham helped bring the project to fruition.

Lyme's new inshore RNLI lifeboat had a busy time immediately it arrived in the late 1960s. On 7 June 1967, three days before Simon Wingfield Digby MP opened its new boat house, the 26-knot rubber vessel made two trips to sea to rescue yachtsmen on the capsized *Wren*. The following day four

Postwar peace and plenty, in 1960, looking north-east across the Cobb harbour to a crowded beach.

were taken from the speedboat *Black Panther*. Then on 25 June 1967 they were out there again in the most newsworthy of this series of rescues. The cabin cruiser *Lilian* had turned over and four people were clinging to the hull. The four males comprised two boys, a 36 year old, and a 70 year old. They told the lifeboat man that a 73-year-old woman was trapped underneath.

Assuming she had drowned, the crew set about righting the vessel, but as the ropes were pulled, Lionel Fisher and Robert 'Nimmer' Jefford managed to force the cabin door off its hinges. *Lilian* lurched sideways, as the lifeboat went into reverse, which caused water to surge out through the door. To the amazement of Fisher and Jefford a lady also floated out and was found to be alive. She owed her life to an air pocket in the upturned hull.

A total of 28 people were rescued during 32 emergency launches before there was a 'shout' too many in circumstances where eagerness overcame experience. No life was at risk other than that of a lifeboat man. Described as 'intrepid and inspirational', Robert Jefford tragically drowned as he tried to put a line on an empty vessel that had broken from its mooring and was being washed ashore in a gale. That was in 1969, and his colleagues were stunned, 'but his spirit lives on'.

Lyme's rescue boat was also called out to several air crashes. On 5 July 1968 a Hunter jet crashed near West Bay. The pilot was able to eject and was rescued but had broken his spine on impact. On 1 May 1970

an RAF Canberra bomber crashed into the sea at Lyme Bay during target-towing trials. Two of the crew were killed and one rescued.

An additional rescue boat, the second fibreglass Dell Quay Dory hull, joined the rubber inflatable for evaluation in 1969. It was 17 feet long, with twin Penta outboard engines capable of 25 knots, and giving a range of over 100 miles. She was provided by the family of Revd G.F. Eyre of Lyme, in his memory, and named *Bob Abbott* for the Lyme coxswain of the first quarter of the twentieth century.

Offshore in Lyme Bay from this time it became a frequent sight to observe what seemed to be the mating habits of oil tankers. Here the great tankers from the Gulf twin-up with a lesser breed. 'Lightening' is the procedure pioneered by Shell in which the partial unloading of crude oil from super-tankers of the 250,000-ton range takes place into smaller vessels. This causes the big ships to rise sufficiently in the water to enable them to enter British harbours. The coast off Lyme Regis was chosen because it is the most sheltered water in the approaches to Britain from the south-west, being protected by the projecting coasts of Start Point and Portland.

I was with Ian Hunter of the *Western Daily Press* on 16 November 1971 as he filed his story for the tabloids. The setting on a hillside above Lyme Regis accentuated the reality that modern lifestyles were no longer restricted to cosmopolitan communities but had spread nationwide. Monkton Wyld, then a

£180-a-term co-educational boarding-school, had been raided by drugs squad officers. They questioned the 61 pupils and took away 'various substances'. Some pupils were also allegedly interviewed about sexual activities and the diary of a 14-year-old girl was removed. The story bounced back on 10 December 1971 when 36 parents of the children held a protest meeting at the school, which passed a vote of confidence in the six teachers and expressed 'extreme dismay' at the manner in which police inquiries were carried out.

A more traditional news story, in November 1971, was that customers from the Marshwood Vale had packed the Bottle Inn, Marshwood, to celebrate the retirement of Bill Stevens on his 65th birthday. They gave him a cheque for £124 and a specially bound book with hundreds of tributes. He had been a baker's roundsman in the Vale since 1921 when he delivered bread from a pony and trap. Mrs R.B. Briscoe of the Mothers' Union told him: 'By your self-less loyal service you have achieved the status of an ambassador of peace and goodwill. No crowned head or prime minister could wish for higher praise.'

A rough-cut piece of timber, set in the blue-lias stone wall of a Coombe Street house, in Lyme Regis, was claimed in 1972 as Britain's oldest postbox. It is set beside the bottom left-hand corner of a downstairs window and is the size of half a railway sleeper. There are both horizontal and upright slots. The latter, the top one, was for the benefit of those on horseback. Originally this upper slot was horizontal but it was re-cut into a vertical one for ease of its mounted users.

One of the strangest stories to unfold in Lyme's countryside concerns murdered dissident Georgi Ivanov Markov (1929–78) who was born in Sofia and is buried in Whitchurch Canonicorum churchyard. His stone records that the novelist and playwright died 'In the cause of freedom' and was 'Bulgaria's most revered dissident'. On one side of the stone the

The Cold War warrior with words from Sofia, who failed to find safety as a political refugee, lies in Whitchurch Canonicorum churchyard.

wording is in English and the other Bulgarian. Although in exile, based in London, Markov continued to be well known inside his homeland for a series of revelatory radio programmes, on the BBC World Service and for the West German-based Radio Free Europe.

The Russian KGB is said to have provided Bulgaria's secret agents with the means for implementing Bulgarian Community Party general secretary Tudor Zhivkov's execution order on the émigré broadcaster in September 1978. As he waited for a bus on Waterloo Bridge an assassin brushed against him and prodded his right thigh with a gas gun disguised as an umbrella. This injected a pin-head sized pellet containing a lethal quantity of the toxic poison ricin, extracted from castor-oil seeds.

His widow, Annabel Dilke, was from West Dorset and they had a daughter, Sasha. Closure of a kind came for the family in 1991 when Bulgarian President Zhelyu Zhelev paid homage, in the pouring rain, beside the grave. 'This crime was a great shame to our country,' he said.

For two years running, in 1979 and 1980, fine-voiced Richard Fox of Lyme Regis was voted World Champion Town Crier. The town's other unlikely export of 1980 was its railway station. Like so many others after the wielding of Beeching's axe it

Modern martyr Georgi Markov, assassinated with a ricin pellet on Waterloo Bridge, died on 11 September 1978.

Richard Fox crying for England as he prepares to fly the flag with British Airways in 1979.

World-record-holding Town Crier Richard Fox from Lyme Regis on arrival in New Orleans.

was demolished but it found a new home at Alresford, near Winchester. The Mid-Hants Railway reopened on 22 March 1980 and the Edwardian timber buildings and signs from the Dorset seaside were back in the authentic atmosphere of steam working.

There was an inshore drama at Lyme Regis on 11 September 1984. Portland Coastguard received a 999 call that 'some persons had been cut off by the tide at Black Beach groynes and bodies could be seen in the water.' The secretary of the Lifeboat Station at Lyme received the message at 6.52p.m. Maroons were fired – this was before the time of universal bleepers – and at seven o'clock the relief Atlantic-21 rigid inflatable was launched with John Hodder at the helm.

The wind was a light north-westerly, force 3 to 4, largely blocked by the cliffs and causing only a slight sea. High water was due at nine o'clock. Full speed was maintained until the lifeboat reached the area but here, due to the groynes, the sea was 'sweeping in from seaward in a confused manner' with waves eight to ten feet high. Three people and a dog were stranded by the rising tide at the end of the groyne, standing on stone steps below the sea wall, and had found themselves trapped between the sea below and a sheer wall above. Here a policeman was leaning over but too far out of reach to give them a hand.

Offshore there were two motionless bodies floating in the water some 20 feet from the sea wall. John Hodder decided that the bodies in the water, if still alive, were at most risk and should be rescued first. The lifeboat manoeuvred towards them using full power from both engines in an extreme arc to try to cope with the confused sea. The two bodies, of a man and a woman, were hauled aboard. Though they 'appeared lifeless, crew members Robert Irish and James Thomas at once administered first aid and resuscitation and continued doing so throughout.'

Hodder then realised that they had to lift the other three off the head of the groyne, in rising water and failing light, as they were now in imminent danger of being swept off by the sea. The lifeboat came in 'using the full range of direction and power' with the stern being held between the steps and the end of the groyne. The typescript I am quoting from, a contemporary account supplied by the Royal National Lifeboat Institution, captures the triumph and the tragedy:

Two males appeared to be suffering from exhaustion and the woman indicated with some despair that she could not leave the dog behind. The helmsman was unable to hold the lifeboat in position for more than a few seconds at a time and had to make eight approaches before all three had been successfully heaved aboard by crew member Paul Watson. The policeman above, meanwhile, had been able to grasp the dog's leash and haul it up the sea wall.

All three survivors were wrapped in thermal sheets and attempts made to warm them by the crew members. The casualties all had to be carried ashore to the waiting ambulance, where the Lifeboat Station honorary medical advisor pronounced two dead and the other three suffering from exposure. The lifeboat made one more trip to the scene to recover a picnic basket and haversack belonging to the casualties.

Minor damage had been sustained to the bow of the lifeboat but this was repaired with a patch and the boat was washed down and re-housed at 7.30p.m. John Hodder has been awarded the RNLI's bravery award and crewmen Paul Watson, Robert Irish and James Thomas have received letters of appreciation.

Fossils also continued to make news with the discovery that the world's oldest moth lived at Lyme Regis 180 million years ago. The specimen loitered in the Natural History Museum in South Kensington, London, for 20 years without anyone knowing. It was locked inside a lump of calcareous mudstone in the Jackson collection, formed by an amateur geologist, which was given to the museum in 1966. Examination of the stone was made by Paul Whalley who made what he called 'a lucky break' in splitting the stone open.

The discovery, announced on 17 February 1985, was named Archaeolepis, meaning 'ancient scales', for the covering of its wings. It easily took the record, being more than 40 million years earlier than the current holder, which was from Russia. Lyme's fossil moth has its closest living relatives in insects of the miscropterygidea group, which include caddis-flies.

On 10 January 1992, listeners to the 'Today' programme on Radio 4 were treated to Nellie Templeton, in her eighties, playing the music for silent films in the Regent Theatre at Lyme Regis. She continued doing so in the 1990s just as she had in the 1920s. Her lush piano mood renderings are entirely from memory and played without looking at the keyboard. This was not only so that she followed each frame of the film but came about because of the total darkness of the early picture houses which caused her to learn to play blind.

The search for a missing person turned into a murder hunt on 11 March 1992. The body of Down's syndrome sufferer Jo Ramsden (1969–91), who disappeared from an adult training centre in Bridport on 9 April 1991, was discovered in woodland at Raymond's Hill, Wootton Fitzpaine, on the summit above Lyme Regis, by Forestry Commission workers. She had last been seen crossing the road in Bridport with 'a young man in a bright patterned jumper' and her decomposed remains were found, accompanied by a Liverpool football bag and multi-coloured tracksuit of the type she had been wearing at the time of her disappearance.

There was the happier note from underwater with the discovery of a 65-foot reef of sunset coral, two

Detail of a slippage, across the Spittles from the golf course down to the sea, looking eastwards in 1985.

Cliff Cottage (left, since righted), *having landslipped on 6 April 1963, in a view north-eastwards from Stile Lane to Bell Cliff and the Buddle estuary* (top right).

miles off Lyme Regis, which is only the third that is known around Britain's coast. The others are in Plymouth Sound and off Lundy Island. The species, dependent upon warm water, is at the northern end of its range in the southern British Isles.

The water in Lyme Bay was far from warm on the Monday afternoon of 20 March 1993. Two instructors, eight sixth-formers from Plymouth and their teacher had set off in canoes from a Lyme Regis activity centre shortly after 10.00 hours. They paddled eastwards and were then intending to turn inshore, to land at Charmouth, with 13.00 being given as the estimated time of arrival.

Nothing was done about their failure to reach land and Portland Coastguards were unaware of any canoeists out at sea until they received a radio call from the West Bay fishing boat *Spanish Eyes* at 14.43: 'Portland, we've picked up an empty canoe.' At 14.58 the Coastguards established that a party had left Lyme five hours earlier. A Land Rover was sent to coastal viewpoints to try to make visual contact. They saw nothing. Almost an hour later, at 15.51, the Coastguards scrambled the first of two Royal Navy Sea King rescue helicopters from RNAS Portland. They arrived on the scene, about 17 miles north-west from their base, at 16.08. Coastguards then launched Lyme's Atlantic 21 inshore lifeboat at 16.11, and a rescue team from All Hallows public school also headed towards the search area.

Meanwhile, at 16.29, the St Alban's Adventure Centre in Lyme identified the canoe recovered by the Bridport fishing boat, and confirmed that it belonged to the group from Southway Comprehensive School, Plymouth. A yellow Royal Air Force Wessex rescue helicopter was scrambled from RAF Chivenor in North Devon. At 17.17 HMS *Beaver* sent her Lynx helicopter to join the aerial search.

By 17.38 the Lyme lifeboat had found survivors and was hauling two adults aboard – alive though suffering from hypothermia – who were taken to West Bay, from where a helicopter took them to hospital. At 17.43 a Sea King picked up another canoeist, a mile east of Lyme Regis, followed by three others by 17.55. They were delivered to Weymouth General Hospital at 18.00. Minutes later, at 18.04, the RAF Wessex helicopter reported that it had picked up four more.

Finally, at 18.44, the second Sea King picked up the last canoeist, who was still breathing, nearly nine hours after they set off and eight hours after they got into difficulties. Questions were asked:

How was it they went to sea without notifying the Coastguards or carrying a marine-band radio for just such an emergency? Had they undertaken capsize drill? Why had non-arrival at Charmouth not been reported when they failed to come into sight at 13.00? On the credit side, wetsuits and lifejackets were being worn, and distress flares carried, though none appears

to have been fired. Had the helicopters been sent at the earliest opportunity?

The prolonged nature of the search took its toll. Four teenagers were pulled from the sea either dead or dying and were named as Simon Dunne (16), Claire Langley (16), Dean Sayer (17), and Rachel Walker (16).

On land there were also problems between Lyme and Charmouth. Coastal erosion, accelerated by huge storms in 1982, caused Lyme Regis Golf Club to re-design its course. The eventual solution was to use its practice holes as the course's second and third holes and re-number the rest of the course after its former fourteenth and fifteenth holes had 'gone off to sea'. Dorset County Council then bought a strip of club land in order to reinstate a lost section of coastal footpath above National Trust land at the Spittles and Black Ven. All this sounds rational and inevitable, in the circumstances, but had generated 'the town's best row for years'. *The Times* reported on 28 June 1994:

The chairman and the president of Lyme Regis Golf Club have resigned and the club captain's locker has been filled with rotting rubbish because of the conflict over how to replace two holes. Members had to decide whether to use their two practice holes to make the course up to 18 holes, or to build two new ones. 'A certain amount of acrimony ensued,' one member said yesterday. 'It is all very sad and the atmosphere at the club has been pretty tense.'

Robin Young went on to report that 71-year-old president Ron Baker and chairman Walter Hepworth, aged 72, had been forced out of office by a campaign of 'hate notes' on the club's notice-board. Then the captain, Harry Austin, found his locker had been forced open and filled with the contents of a litter bin. Arguments raged until the eventual decision and resignations. As one Austin smoothed those troubled waters, another tackled disputes in the town, with Barbara Austin becoming Lyme's first lady Mayor in 1994. She continued in post until 1997 and brought, as John Fowles put it, 'benign rule', in place of strife.

The man who could smile at it all was fossil hunter Chris Moore from the Old Forge Fossil Shop in Broad Street. He found a superb ichthyosaurus skull – one of Mary Anning's 'fish-lizards' – in a landslip on the other side of Charmouth. It began to emerge from the cliff after the same storms that claimed the golfing greens. Chris passed these every day, for weeks, as he set off to resume the careful excavation of his find. He then spent a year doing microsurgery; meticulously preparing it for display. His two business partners, Dave Costin and John Mould, continued the outdoor vigil and returned to the undercliff of Golden Cap to search for more of the body.

Details of the find were added to the submissions that saw Devon and Dorset's Jurassic coast being

*Looking south-west over the outer breakwater
of the Cobb to Devonshire Head and
Seven Rock Point, in 1988.*

A calm day in 1998, looking southwards to the Cobb harbour at low tide.

Guildhall cupola and modern sea defences, north-eastwards to the Marine Theatre (right), *in 1997.*

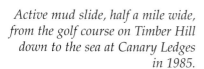

Active mud slide, half a mile wide, from the golf course on Timber Hill down to the sea at Canary Ledges in 1985.

The former London Inn, now a guest-house, on the corner near the northern end of Church Street, looking south-east in 1997.

North-eastwards across the Square, from Bell Cliff, to the Pilot Boat, Bridge Street (centre), Rock Point Inn and Cobb Gate Fish Bar, in 1997.

successfully listed as England's first natural World Heritage Site, by the United Nations Educational, Scientific and Cultural Organization in December 2001. Chris Moore proudly told Edward Oldfield of the *Western Daily Press* about his find:

It is a massive specimen and one of the biggest and best preserved complete skulls ever found. It is also three-dimensional, so you can see just how mean a creature this was. The ichthyosaur looked a bit like a dolphin but it had many very sharp teeth – and was much less friendly.

Offshore, a reminder of the present perils of sea came on Sunday 10 June 1995, when brothers Tom and Les Davies and their friend Andrew Sparks went out fishing from the Cobb. They had taken their new 14-foot boat on its maiden voyage. The day ended with an air-sea search across Lyme Bay, into the English Channel, and continued until the middle of the week when it was abandoned by the Coastguards.

Campanologists come to Lyme 'from all over Britain and beyond' to 'ring or just to hear the peal' of ten bells which are of the finest quality. The historic eight were recast by John Taylor and Company at Loughborough for the coronation of Queen Elizabeth II in 1953. The ninth and tenth, made at Whitechapel Bell Foundry, were delivered in 1988, courtesy of a Sea King helicopter supplied by the Royal Naval Air Station at Culdrose. In 1995 the ringers at St Michael's Parish Church achieved the world's longest peal of 'Surprise Royal' when they took almost 12 hours – without a break of any kind – to complete 20,000 changes. The 'town's top ten belfry' comprises:

TREBLE, named Roger, in memory of bell-ringer Revd Roger Keeley; the old starting bell from Kings Cross Station (musical note B). Weight 3 cwt 1 stone 13 pounds.

SECOND, named Stedman, in memory of bell-ringer George Stedman Morris (note A). Weight 3 cwt 2 stone 2 pounds.

THIRD, named Anthony, 'in memorium M.H.E.T. A.A.G.B.' (note G). Weight 3 cwt 3 stone 8 pounds.

FOURTH, named Edwin, for Edwin Eglon, parish clerk from 1931 to 1951 (note F#). Weight 4 cwt 0 stone 11 pounds.

FIFTH, named George, for Revd George Barlow, vicar from 1883 to 1887, who is also commemorated by the chancel screen (note E). Weight 4 cwt 1 stone 13 pounds.

SIXTH, named Carew, for Revd Charles Carew Cox, vicar from 1927 to 1954 (note D). Weight 4 cwt 3 stone 13 pounds.

SEVENTH, named Cuthbert, in memory of bell-ringer Cuthbert W.H. Powell (note C). Weight 5 cwt 0 stone 3 pounds.

EIGHTH, named Michael for Saint Michael, and inscribed for Revd Frederick Parry Hodges, vicar, Robert Hillman, mayor, and John Church and George Roberts, churchwardens (note B). Weight 6 cwt 0 stone 1 pound.

NINTH, named Elizabeth, for Queen Elizabeth II, having been re-cast in coronation year, 1953 (note A). Weight 7 cwt 1 stone 23 pounds.

TENTH, named John, in memory of John Davy Hodder (note G). Weight 10 cwt 3 stone 18 pounds.

The vicar, Revd Murray Dell, told me that Michael carries a poignant inscription summing up the perpetual prayer not only of those who enter St Michael's Church but all who live on Lyme's unstable geology. It should be the town's motto: 'O Sea, Spare Me.'

Many thought they were heading that way when, according to *The Times*, 'furniture trembled' in Lyme Regis, at 00.53 hours British Summer Time on Monday 23 September 2002. Nationally there were 15,000 phone calls to the emergency services from people fearing 'a plane crash or terrorist attack' or, in one case, 'World War Three'. The shudder lasted for 15 seconds and was followed by a lesser shock at 04.32 hours that morning.

Reassurance came from seismologist Roger Musson of the British Geological Survey. Pressures from a south-easterly shift of the Eurasian tectonic plate, resisted by northward movement by the African plate, had caused an earthquake which registered 4.8 on the Richter scale (equivalent of 1,000 tonnes of TNT). Their timings are recorded on the Universal Time Clock at 23.53 hours Greenwich Mean Time which changes the official date of the occurrence to Sunday 22 September. Its epicentre was at Brick Kiln Lane, Gornal Wood, near Dudley in the West Midlands, where mining subsidence had seemed the likely culprit as chimneys and a church spire collapsed and walls cracked.

Lyme shared the wake-up call on 'the night that Middle England rocked'. Were it to have happened under West Dorset, in what turned out to be the wettest autumn on record, it would certainly have triggered landslips or worse. 'It is written in the Bible that there will be earthquakes in diverse place,' Vi Robinson of Dudley told a reporter. 'This is God's wake-up call to mankind, especially in hedonistic, materialistic, godless Britain.' On the other hand, when it does happen in Lyme, creationists will have to watch their backs as fossil hunters enjoy a field-day on the beach.

Sparkling sea, westwards from Broad Ledge groyne to 1994-built sea defences and the Guildhall cupola in 1996.

Anchor set-piece on blue lias stone setts beside the Square in a view over Cobb Gate Jetty, south-westwards, to the Cobb in 1998.

Above: *Between the breakers near the south-western end of Marine Parade, looking across to the Cobb in 1998.*

Cottage fire, near Horn Bridge, as a reminder of that age-old risk in the mid-1990s.

Gun guard for 1994-built sea defences beside the Square, pointing eastwards to the highest cliff on the South Coast – Golden Cap – in 1998.

Ventilation shaft to a 1994-built sewage collection tank beside the promenade extension across Long Ledge, looking north-eastwards to Cain's Folly (right) in 1997.

*Mouth of the Buddle as reconstructed in 1994,
with huge boulders of imported geology,
in a view eastwards to Church Beach
and Golden Cap (right) in 1998.*

*Westwards up the back street between Fudge Kitchen Tea Rooms and Bell Cliff Restaurant,
towards Broad Street in 1997.*

Subscribers

Michael Allman, Kidderminster

Bob Anderson, Haye Farm, Lyme Regis

Angela and Derrick Bott, Minehead, Somerset

Roz Bound, Ontario, Canada

Raymond W. Boynton, Lyme Regis

Olivia Buckley, Reading, Berkshire

Mr Brian Chambers, Lyme Regis, Dorset

John and Mary Cheetham, Chesterfield, Derbyshire

Joan and Dave Collett, Lyme Regis

Jenny Waldron and Rob Cross, Lyme Regis

Jeffrey Ellwood and Toni Delaney-Ellwood, Uplyme House, Uplyme

Mrs S. Dunford, Dover, Kent

Mr Tom Eaton, Candlemas Cottage, Lyme Regis

Mr John Eaton, Timber Vale Caravan Park, Lyme Regis

Sarah Elizabeth Edwards, Wigan

Barrie and Maureen Etherington, Lyme Regis

Christopher G. Finch, Redbourn, Hertfordshire

Miss Sarah E. Ford, Lyme Regis, Dorset

Prop Teresa Fowler (née Ody), House of Flowers, Broad Street, Lyme Regis

Sara J. Frampton,

David and Marion Gale, Lyme Regis/Reading

Jonathan Galloway, Lyme Regis, Dorset

Antonio and Julie Gravili, Lyme Regis, Dorset

G. and K.N. Hall, Stakeford, Northumberland

Clive Hamilton Pullen, Watford, Hertfordshire

Mr and Mrs Jack Hansen

Mrs Katherine Harvey (née Hansen), Chippenham, Berkshire

David J. Haskins, Lyme Regis, Dorset

Geoffrey J. Hatton, Lyme Regis, Dorset

Mrs Jayne Hawes, Uplyme

Robin M. Heslop, Uplyme, Dorset

Mrs F.L. Hopkins, Lyme Regis, Dorset

Robert Janvey, Portland

Dr Deborah Jenkins, Lyme Regis

Martin J. Kendrick

Atticus, Zeb and Xuxa Kidd, Lyme Regis

Peter J. Lacey, Lyme Regis, Dorset

Dr Graham A. Loud, Lyme Regis

Ex Mayoress Christine Lovell, Lyme Regis

Vic and Lesley Luck, Lyme Regis, Dorset

Neal F.R. Luxton, Lyme Regis, Dorset

Andrew Mason, Uplyme

Mrs Gillian Menzies, Lyme Regis, Dorset

Jane Mitchell, Wrington, Somerset

Jim Morgan, Lyme Regis

Liz and Guy Patey, Chard, Somerset

Rachel Pike, The Orchard Country Hotel, Lyme Regis

Ann Porter, Lyme Regis, Dorset

Christopher Powell, Llandaff, Cardiff

Neil and Heather Pullinger, Lyme Regis, Dorset

Janet Ragless (née Mason), Uplyme

Kerrigan Redman, Lyme Regis

Tony F. Rice, Lyme Regis, Dorset

Carol E. Robson, Lyme Regis, Dorset

Robin and Julia Sargeant, Lyme Regis, Dorset

Mark Seaton, Brisbane, Australia

Astra Seaton, Lyme Regis, Dorset

Astra Seaton-Cox, Bishop Sutton, Somerset

Simes, Lyme Regis

Maggie Snow, Black Rock, Victoria, Australia

Richard and Margaret Snowsill, Lyme Regis

Christine A. Stone, Shepton Mallet, Somerset

T. Studley, Lyme Regis, Dorset

Derek Taylor, Dove Cottage, Lyme Regis

Scott Taylor, Lyme Regis, Dorset

Mr Laurence and Mrs Deirdre Taylor, Lyme Regis, Dorset

Michael and Jane Templeman

Pat and David Venes, Lyme Regis, Dorset

Paul and Ruth Wason, Lyme Regis, Dorset

Luke Wason, Lyme Regis, Dorset

Rachel Wason, Lyme Regis, Dorset

George W. Wood, Lyme Regis, Dorset

Rhoen Young, Wingfield, Wiltshire

Community Histories

The Book of Addiscombe • Canning & Clyde Road Residents Association & Friends
The Book of Addiscombe, Vol. II • Canning & Clyde Road Residents Association & Friends
The Book of Axminster with Kilmington • Les Berry
and Gerald Gosling
The Book of Bampton • Caroline Seward
The Book of Barnstaple • Avril Stone
The Book of Barnstaple, Vol. II • Avril Stone
The Book of The Bedwyns • The Bedwyn History Society
The Book of Bickington • Stuart Hands
Blandford Forum: A Millennium Portrait • Blandford Town Council
The Book of Bramford • Bramford Local History Group
The Book of Breage & Germoe • Stephen Polglase
The Book of Bridestowe • R. Cann
The Book of Bridport • Rodney Legg
The Book of Brixham • Frank Pearce
The Book of Buckfastleigh • Sandra Coleman
The Book of Buckland Monachorum & Yelverton • Pauline Hemery
The Book of Carharrack • Carharrack Old Cornwall Society
The Book of Carshalton • Stella Wilks and Gordon Rookledge
The Parish Book of Cerne Abbas • Vale and Vale
The Book of Chagford • Ian Rice
The Book of Chapel-en-le-Frith • Mike Smith
*The Book of Chittlehamholt with
Warkleigh & Satterleigh* • Richard Lethbridge
The Book of Chittlehampton • Various
The Book of Colney Heath • Bryan Lilley
The Book of Constantine • Moore and Trethowan
The Book of Cornwood & Lutton • Compiled by the People of the Parish
The Book of Creech St Michael • June Small
The Book of Cullompton • Compiled by the People of the Parish
The Book of Dawlish • Frank Pearce
*The Book of Dulverton, Brushford,
Bury & Exebridge* • Dulverton & District Civic Society
The Book of Dunster • Hilary Binding
The Book of Edale • Gordon Miller
The Ellacombe Book • Sydney R. Langmead
The Book of Exmouth • W.H. Pascoe
The Book of Grampound with Creed • Bane and Oliver
The Book of Hayling Island & Langstone • Rogers
The Book of Helston • Jenkin with Carter
The Book of Hemyock • Clist and Dracott
The Book of Herne Hill • Patricia Jenkyns
The Book of Hethersett • Hethersett Society Research Group
The Book of High Bickington • Avril Stone
The Book of Ilsington • Dick Wills
The Book of Kingskerswell • Carsewella Local History Group
The Book of Lamerton • Ann Cole & Friends
Lanner, A Cornish Mining Parish • Sharron
Schwartz and Roger Parker
The Book of Leigh & Bransford • Malcolm Scott
The Book of Litcham with Lexham & Mileham • Litcham Historical & Amenity Society
The Book of Loddiswell • Reg and Betty Sampson
The New Book of Lostwithiel • Barbara Fraser
The Book of Lulworth • Rodney Legg
The Book of Lustleigh • Joe Crowdy
The Book of Lyme Regis • Rodney Legg
The Book of Manaton • Compiled by the People of the Parish
The Book of Markyate • Markyate Local History Society
The Book of Mawnan • Mawnan Local History Group
The Book of Meavy • Pauline Hemery
The Book of Minehead with Alcombe • Binding and Stevens
The Book of Morchard Bishop • Jeff Kingaby

FURTHER TITLES

The Book of Newdigate • John Callcut
The Book of Nidderdale • Nidderdale Musuem Society
The Book of Northlew with Ashbury • Northlew History Group
The Book of North Newton • Robins and Robins
The Book of North Tawton • Baker, Hoare and Shields
The Book of Nynehead • Nynehead & District History Society
The Book of Okehampton • Radford and Radford
The Book of Paignton • Frank Pearce
The Book of Penge, Anerley & Crystal Palace • Peter Abbott
The Book of Peter Tavy with Cudlipptown • Peter Tavy Heritage Group
The Book of Pimperne • Jean Coull
The Book of Plymtree • Tony Eames
The Book of Porlock • Denis Corner
Postbridge – The Heart of Dartmoor • Reg Bellamy
The Book of Priddy • Albert Thompson
The Book of Princetown • Dr Gardner-Thorpe
The Book of Rattery • By the People of the Parish
The Book of St Day • Joseph Mills and Paul Annear
The Book of Sampford Courtenay
with Honeychurch • Stephanie Pouya
The Book of Sculthorpe • Gary Windeler
The Book of Seaton • Ted Gosling
The Book of Sidmouth • Ted Gosling and Sheila Luxton
The Book of Silverton • Silverton Local History Society
The Book of South Molton • Jonathan Edmunds
The Book of South Stoke with Midford • Edited by Robert Parfitt
South Tawton & South Zeal with Sticklepath • Radford and Radford
The Book of Sparkwell with Hemerdon & Lee Mill • Pam James
The Book of Staverton • Pete Lavis
The Book of Stithians • Stithians Parish History Group
The Book of Stogumber, Monksilver, Nettlecombe
& Elworthy • Maurice and Joyce Chidgey
The Book of Studland • Rodney Legg
The Book of Swanage • Rodney Legg
The Book of Tavistock • Gerry Woodcock
The Book of Thorley • Sylvia McDonald and Bill Hardy
The Book of Torbay • Frank Pearce
Uncle Tom Cobley & All:
Widecombe-in-the-Moor • Stephen Woods
The Book of Watchet • Compiled by David Banks
The Book of West Huntspill • By the People of the Parish
Widecombe-in-the-Moor • Stephen Woods
The Book of Williton • Michael Williams
The Book of Witheridge • Peter and Freda Tout and John Usmar
The Book of Withycombe • Chris Boyles
Woodbury: The Twentieth Century Revisited • Roger Stokes
The Book of Woolmer Green • Compiled by the People of the Parish

For details of any of the above titles or if you are
interested in writing your own history, please contact: Commissioning Editor Community Histories,
Halsgrove House, Lower Moor Way, Tiverton Business Park, Tiverton, Devon EX16 6SS, England;
email: naomic@halsgrove.com